T0355044

OTHER WORKS BY THIS AUTHOR

The Shadow of Kukulkan
Beyond El Camino Del Diablo; Beyond the Devil's Highway
The Way of Saint James; Journey to America
Athirst In Spirit
Sandals
Walk In The Light
Rio Viejo: Some Memories of Vietnam
Do You Believe In Miracles?
(Co-authored with Angela Lopez)
Escape From The Shadow

RIO VIEJO

SOME MEMORIES OF Vietnam

EUGENE L. SIERRAS, JR.

Order this book online at www.trafford.com
or email orders@trafford.com

Most Trafford titles are also available at major online book retailers.

Print information available on the last page.

ISBN: 978-1-6987-1882-8 (sc)
ISBN: 978-1-6987-1883-5 (e)

Library of Congress Control Number: 2025902263

Trafford rev.   02/07/2025

 www.trafford.com
North America & international
toll-free: 844-688-6899 (USA & Canada)
fax: 812 355 4082

A NAVY FLYER'S CREED

I am a United States Navy flyer.

My countrymen built the best airplane in the world and entrusted it to me.

They trained me to fly it.

I will use it to the absolute limit of my power.

With my fellow pilots, air crews, and deck crews, my plane and I will do anything necessary to carry out our tremendous responsibilities.

I will always remember we are part of an unbeatable combat team - the United States Navy.

When the going is fast and rough, I will not falter.

I will be uncompromising in every blow I strike.

I will be humble in victory.

I am a United States Navy flyer.

I have dedicated myself to my country, with its many millions of all races, colors, and creeds. They and their way of life are worth of my greatest protective effort.

I ask the help of God in making that effort great enough.

One of the documents from several works of history of the United States Navy in World War Two. I read and was inspired when I read this as a youth and am inspired by it to this day.

ABOUT THE AUTHOR

Eugene Sierras was born in Tucson, Arizona. He attended local schools, and graduated from the University of Arizona in 1964.

He was immediately called to active duty with the United States Navy and served until his retirement in 1986. During his service he served on various ships and fighter squadrons.

After retirement from the navy, he completed a second career with the Arizona Department of Public Safety.

He currently lives in Tucson, Arizona with his wife.

A NAVY FLYER'S PSALM 23

The Lord is my flight leader: I shall not want.

Yea, though I fly into the valley of the shadow of death,

Shall I fear no evil:

For I am on thy wing and thou leadest me into and out of harms way.

Thou guidest me with the voice of CATC and preparest a ready deck

In the presence of mine enemies.

Thou bringest me safely home and anointest my head with oil;

My cup runneth over.

Surely goodness and mercy shall follow me all the days of my life:

Ant I will dwell in the house of the Lord forever.

LT Eugene Sierras

USS Enterprise (CVAN65)

May 1968

INTRODUCTION TO THE 2015 REVISION

April 11, 2015

I updated RIO VIEJO to complete the details of the events I first wrote about by taking advantage of the latest developments of the internet. The internet not only afforded me the ability to research extensive information that either was unavailable to me initially or permitted me access to several individuals whose friendship, knowledge and willingness to share with me documents increased my understanding and knowledge of the details of my experiences I wrote about in the first printing. When I began to write my first novel, The Shadow of Kukulkan, I chose as the main character a recently retired US Navy Chief Petty Officer who served on Swift Boats in Vietnam. I did so because I was peripherally involved in a series of events which occurred involving Swift Boats off the coast of the Demilitarized Zone (DMZ) between North and South Vietnam in June of 1968. This experience stayed in my memory through many years. I never was able to learn the details of that night until beginning research on Kukulkan led me to contact the Swift Boat Sailors Association. Finally, after several years, I began to learn more of what happened on that night although the final writing of the Navy's history of those events remains in the future. This was one of the experiences I encountered and wrote about without full information of all the details involved. There were others.

I returned from my final tour in Fighter Squadron Ninety-Six (VF 96) aboard the USS Enterprise (CVAN 65) during the summer of 1969. I remained in the Navy and was assigned to instructor duty at the Naval Air Technical Training Center in Glynco. I was married for two years to Juley Wainwright with a 15-month old son (Eugene Edward or Eddy). I was separated from my bride for most of the two years we were married and for most of my son's young life. I was anxious to devote as much time as possible to my young family and to my next assignment as a RIO Instructor at the same command from which I received my wings in January of 1967, the same month and year I married. I "got on with my life," busy with my future and family. I did not look back at my Vietnam experience. It wasn't until after I retired from the Navy, and about to retire from my second career with the Arizona Department of Public Safety, that I began to reflect back on those days which were filled with so much activity and emotion. It was this juncture that I began to reflect on the past and to write down my experience.

Since I completed RIO VIEJO and its subsequent revisions prior to this one, I have self-published three novels: The Shadow of Kukulkan, Command Screen, and Beyond El Camino Del Diablo, Beyond the Devil's Highway. As a result of this experience, I became familiar with the advent of the "eBook," initially with Amazon's Kindle. I intend to publish this memoir as an eBook on Kindle not so much to sell copies but to make it available to future grandchildren and great grandchildren who someday may be curious about what Great Grandpa did back in the day. My father introduced me to genealogy after I retired from the Navy and I came to realized how much work and effort it took to find and research family history. Imagine how much easier it will be for future genealogists who have digitized historical records to work from. It is with that purpose in mind that I complete this effort. If any of my grandchildren take an interest in it I will consider it a success. If not, that's fine as well. At least these words will remain long after I have embarked on my final WestPac cruise.

Tucson, Arizona

April 2007

I'm reprinting "Rio Viejo" this year. I have one copy of the ten I originally printed.

I've distributed copies to selected friends and family members. When I sent LT Col Dale Ackles, a good friend with whom I served on the staff of the Joint Special Operations Command, he distributed it to several other individuals who circulated the copy to numerous others. Dale advised me he learned that at least twenty individuals, some retired from the military and some still on active duty, recommended I forward a copy to the Navy's "Veteran's History" project. I wanted a few more copies available.

I inadvertently omitted two paragraphs from the first printing in my attempt to get "Rio Viejo" into print for my father. I have corrected this oversight and hopefully some of the typographical errors in the first printing. I noticed that Dad was deteriorating in the late summer of 2002. The family planned an annual picnic in the environs of the Tucson Mountain Park as we did every year when the weather became cool enough to gather outdoors. Our extended family numbers thirty individuals when all are together.

I wanted to present Dad with a copy at that gathering. He was my inspiration and my mentor when I was young. He flew from Tucson to Newport in October of 1964 when I received my commission as an Ensign, United States Naval Reserve. He was also the first one I called from Philadelphia in 1979 when I learned by reading a copy of Navy Times that I was promoted to Commander, USN. Unfortunately, Dad never saw "Rio Viejo." He passed away before it was available.

It is to his memory that I dedicate this second printing. He was a member of "The Greatest Generation" who willingly endured hardship in defense of his country and did so without expectation of anything other than the chance to do his duty. He never spoke of "Honor, Duty, Country." He was a man given to few words. However, he lived his life in a manner that left no room for doubt that he passionately believed in "God, Honor, Duty, Country and Family" not as some symbolic precept but as a living legacy of his life and achievement.

Thanks, Dad. Tucson, Arizona

CONTENTS

CHAPTER ONE

Vietnam

———————

THERE ARE OVER FIFTY-EIGHT THOUSAND NAMES OF THOSE KILLED OR missing on the Vietnam Memorial in Washington, D.C. The names which are inscribed there represent countless stories of young men who served their country when asked to do so and who never returned. Many who did return did so with broken bodies and spirits. It is to their memory that I dedicate my efforts in rewriting my recollections of my limited participation in that war.

I volunteered for service in Vietnam for many reasons. I requested training as a RIO and that included the assignment of service in South East Asia. I also believed my government when it stated that if South Vietnam fell there was a highly likely possibility that Laos, Cambodia, Thailand and Burma would also fall spreading communist control throughout that part of the world, referred to as the "Domino Theory." Similar to many things about Vietnam, it never came to pass.

I believed I needed to punch my ticket for my birthright of being an American. I have always been grateful to have been born an American. I do not want to live under any other government. I realize that this government, comparable to any other institution which man has evolved, is not perfect. I have lived under it for over eighty years and I am more familiar with its imperfections. I am also aware of its promise and honestly believe that it is the best system in which to live. I agree with Winston Churchill's oft repeated quote: "…it has been said that democracy is the worst form of Government except for all those other forms that have been tried from time to time...."[1]

The decade of the sixties were during the dark days of the Cold War. I always understood, in a way, why some people were protesting the war and doing everything they could to avoid service in it. I knew by instinct, as well as reflection, that if everyone refused to serve it would be inimical to the survival of the United States. How could America survive the existential threat of the Soviet Union and its ambitions to spread communism over the entire globe? I realized that if those in the military refused to do their duty the United States as I knew it would cease to exist.

Those who served their country during this unpopular war bore the burden of duty for which they can be proud. Over two-million, six-hundred, thirty-thousand Americans served in Vietnam. The overwhelming number of these people served with honor. There were some few who dishonored their country by their actions. There were others in high places of the government that brought greater dishonor to themselves, the country, and to the people who served in that conflict by their actions and arrogance of power. I believe the greatest cowards of this war were those in the congress of the United States who failed to discharge their duty and obligations under the Constitution, who were intimidated by President Johnson. I have been able to see this more clearly in hindsight.

My father had served in the Navy during World War II and remained in the Reserves beyond the war retiring as a Master Chief Petty Officer. I remember one night during the Korean War when three of his friends, Naval Reservists in his unit, visited our home one evening and asked if they could speak to him. He invited them in but they asked if they could speak to him outside. My dad told my mother he was going to go around to the side of the house and speak to them

---

[1] Many forms of Government have been tried, and will be tried in this world of sin and woe. No one pretends that democracy is perfect or all-wise. Indeed it has been said that democracy is the worst form of Government except for all those other forms that have been tried from time to time....'
Winston S Churchill, 11 November 1947 www. https://winstonchurchill. org/resources/quotes/the-worst-form-of-government/

under the vineyard. I quietly left the house through the back door and positioned myself in the carport where I could hear my dad and his friends speak but they couldn't see me in the dark. I listened to one of the men as he told dad that they received word that their reserve Construction Battalion was about to be called up and that if called up they would deploy to Korea to help construct military facilities there. I remember my dad's words to the effect that if he were asked to go he would do so. He advised his companions he already arranged his paperwork to ensure his family would be taken care of when he was gone (he was a Yeoman before becoming a Storekeeper so he was thoroughly familiar with the procedures required).

I was frightened at the thought of my dad leaving. I could remember an earlier time when my mother would tell me to go outside and see if he was returning from the Pacific where he served in World War II. I didn't want him to go away again. I was crying softly to myself and couldn't hear the rest of the conversation until they started to say goodbye and threw in a few good-natured remarks when leaving so that everyone parted in a happier frame of mind. It happened that my dad's outfit was not called to active duty as a unit and he never left. He was willing to do so and although he never spoke to me about it I knew he would answer his country's call. I believed it was no less an obligation for me.

It was not until after I retired from my Navy career that I learned Dad was exempt from the draft in World War II. He was the sole support of not only my mother and me but also of my grandmother and two of his nieces, my cousins. His sister died in childbirth after giving birth to his younger niece, Deanne Margaret, and my dad assumed the responsibility of caring for them as well. He did not have to serve. However, he did volunteer to serve and did so in the Pacific Theater having been stationed in the Philippine Islands among other assignments.

One of the great institutions of the United States is its public education system. It didn't make any difference what a child's background was, he or she learned of the country's history and its history became part of their life. My education included American history, which if biased in some respects, led me to appreciate the

3

privilege of freedom and independence. I also have a fondness for philosophy. By the time I received orders to Vietnam, I was twenty six years old. I read Karl Marx and his predecessor, Georg Wilhelm Hegel, during my Philosophy course at the University of Arizona. By the very philosophical tenets that communism was based on, it was obvious to me that it would not endure although I thought at that time that it would not collapse until well into the twenty first century. I also read several histories of Vietnam which made me realize the Vietnamese were a people for at least two thousand years and for much of that time were fighting the Chinese[2]. I didn't believe the premise of a monolithic communism that would cast its shadow over the world although I did genuinely believe that there was a real possibility of a world war which could end our country's existence as I knew it. I came to believe that the American involvement in Vietnam would, at best, be a holding action in a larger Cold War.

The result was, although I was skeptical of the reason for this particular war, I believed it was my duty to serve and the right thing to do. I still believe that way although I will never trust a politician again. I consider Vietnam as the price for living in a democracy such as ours. Although I don't like or want my fate to be determined by greedy, ignorant, and power hungry politicians, in the final analysis I would rather that if it has to be, the politicians be democratically elected Americans and not political commissars, aristocrats, tyrants, or religious fanatics of some other system. In the final analysis, American politicians must still answer to the electorate.

I faced my future experience in Vietnam with as much preparation as I could. I took many preparations to ensure that my family would

---

[2]   Vietnam's long coastal and narrowed lands, rugged mountainous terrains, with two major deltas, were soon home to several different ancient cultures and civilizations. In the north, the Dong Son culture and its indigenous chiefdoms of Van Lang and Âu Lạc flourished by 500 BC. In Central Vietnam, the Sa Huỳnh culture of Austronesian Chamic peoples also thrived. Both were swept away by the Han dynasty expansion from the north, with the Han conquest of Nanyue bringing parts of Vietnam under Chinese rule in 111 BC. In 40 AD, the Trưng sisters led the first uprising of Indigenous tribes and peoples against Chinese domination. www. https://en.wikipedia.org/wiki/History_of_Vietnam

be taken care of if anything happened to me. I also resolved to be as prepared as possible to complete my tour and return. I was aware of the role that luck, good or bad, played, and accepted it as a fact of life.

The memories of my experiences in that war are being written in 2002 some thirty-four to thirty-five years after my service. I believe it's worthwhile to do so. I realize that I have to supplement my memory with research and have some sources available to me including my flight log book, the F4J NATOPS[3] manual, the declassified "Red Baron[4]" reports and many newspaper clippings from that era. My recall is as accurate as I can remember although there will be descriptions of missions that are a composite of several flights.

With the advent of the Internet it has become much easier to learn of organizations of veterans who participated in the Vietnam War and who share experiences and community service. It was through the Internet that I obtained the "Red Baron" Reports under the Freedom of Information Act. It was through the Internet that I was able to purchase a reprinted copy of the F4 NATOPS manual. It was reprinted in China by an American company who previously obtained it from the Navy and made it available to the public. I ordered various aeronautical charts of North Vietnam through a Canadian company via the Internet which allows me to reinforce my memories of that distant country with which I was once remarkably familiar. Some of my memories are forever vivid in my mind. Others are not so clear. There are some missions that I remember but which are a composite of more than one mission. I was only one of over two million Americans who served our country in Vietnam. My part was small. I was proud to serve my country then and I am proud today that I served. If my country ever needed an older man to mount the Phantom to fly and fight for it in the skies, preferably over the enemy's land, I would do so. The Phantom of course has been replaced by newer and better aircraft

---

[3] NATOPS stands for Naval Air Training and Operating Procedures Standardization. It's a program that aims to improve combat readiness and reduce aircraft accidents.

[4] The Navy's Red Baron reports are a series of investigations into the Navy's air-to-air performance during the Vietnam War

crewed by young men who are superbly fit and trained. My best wishes to them and my enduring gratitude for their service to our country.

I recently learned of the "Battle Hymn of the Red River Rats" while surfing the Internet. If the chance presents itself, I recommend the reader listen to it. Below is a quote from one verse:

> *"We flew the Valley and the railroad lines*
> *From Dien Bien Phu to the Cam Pho mines*
> *The price was high and measured in rich red blood.*
> *When tales are told in the halls of fame*
> *When warriors meet you'll hear these names:*
> *Sky Hawk, Crusader, Intruder, Phantom, Thud.*[5]"

---

[5] Battle Hymn of the Red River Rats Erosonic
http://www.erosonic.com › album2 › text2 › ratshymn
Battle Hymn of the Red River Rats. Copyright © 1970 Dick Jonas. All rights reserved. Words and music: Dick Jonas; Enchantment Music/BMI

CHAPTER TWO

Rockville

AVIATION WAS NOT A CENTRAL PART OF MY LIFE WHILE GROWING UP. I do remember my father taking my sister Diane and me to an airshow at Davis-Monthan Air Force Base in the fifties. I was naturally curious about all the aircraft on display and the airman with their spit-shined boots and starched fatigues. What I remember distinctly to this day is the Air Forces' Aerobatic Team, the Thunderbirds, performing in the F100 Super Sabre. Watching them perform their loops and acrobatics kindled a desire in me to fly which never went out although it may have only burned as a dim flicker until my college days.

I was a junior at the University of Arizona when my roommate Dave McVey and I decided to take the Air Force flight exam to see if we could qualify for pilot training. We both passed the written exam. I learned, however, that I had 20/100 vision in my right eye which precluded me from pilot training. The Air Force offered me other programs but I didn't want to participate since I was already in the Navy Reserve and I anticipated serving my active duty requirement in that service. My father served in the Navy during World War II and remained in the Naval Reserve. This of course was during the days of universal military service for young men.

After graduation in 1964 I reported for Navy Officer Candidate School (OCS) in Newport, Rhode Island. It was during the indoctrination presentation from representatives of all warfare specialties in the Navy that I learned of the Naval Flight Officer (NFO) program. I also learned that NFOs flew in quite a variety of naval aircraft including the Phantom where they performed as crewmen in the rear cockpit. I made up my mind at that time that I would fly in the Phantom.

I had to take an indirect path. After completion of OCS I was assigned to a small ship, the USS Rockville (EPCER 851). I was assigned to her via a ten-week Damage Control Assistant (DCA) course and Nuclear, Biological and Chemical Warfare Course at Naval Station Philadelphia.

The Rockville was built during World War II as a "sub chaser," a small anti-submarine platform for service in the North Atlantic which included convoy escort duties. She had a 3"/50 dual purpose gun mounted forward. She also had two 40 mm gun mounts and two depth charge racks on the fantail. She was 184 feet in length, thirty-three feet abeam, and a draft of nine feet, about the same size as an ocean going Minesweeper. Her displacement was 903 tons. Her power plant consisted of two General Motors 900 bhp (brake horsepower or shaft horsepower), twelve cylinder diesel engines. Her initial hull designation was PCE (Patrol Craft Escort).

After the Battle of the Atlantic was successfully decided, Rockville was retrofitted as a hospital ship and re-designated PCER for Patrol Craft Escort Rescue. She was transferred to the Pacific Fleet and assigned to the Third Fleet where her primary mission was to retrieve downed aviators and provide immediate medical treatment. She also had at least one 23-millimeter anti-aircraft battery on her superstructure and was credited with at least one Japanese aircraft kill.

After the war she was decommissioned and was part of the reserve fleet. In October 1951 she was re-commissioned, her armament removed, and fitted with a large sonar dome forward which gave her an effective draft of fifteen feet. She was again redesigned as EPCER for "Experimental Patrol Craft Escort Rescue" and assigned to the United States Naval Observatory. She served with the Naval Observatory in the sixties until just before I reported aboard in January of 1965. She was reassigned to Commander, Naval Surface Forces Atlantic for a classified mission which has since been declassified and about which I can write.

During the Cold War, the Soviet Union developed a strategic nuclear submarine striking force which could deploy into both the Atlantic and Pacific oceans. The Soviet submarines did not have the range the American strategic submarines did so they had to position themselves close to the United States, over the Continental Shelf. The United States developed a system of underwater listening devices, or hydrophones, which were positioned on the Continental Shelf and in the shallow waters in the Norway-Iceland Gap through which the deploying Soviet submarines had to traverse to their stations in the Atlantic. (There were other installations in the world but I was not aware of those.) American observers could not only pinpoint the Soviet submarine's position as she transited thereby making it easier for an American submarine to locate and track her, but learned to identify individual submarines by the characteristic sonic signature each one possessed.

Rockville was fitted with devices that she could tow astern which resembled a fat, short torpedo and which emitted various audio signals which the listening shore stations used to calibrate their listening gear. Other than the Commanding Officer the crew of Rockville was not given specific details of the capability of the noise maker but we always suspected that we could also emulate American submarines as well. Occasionally civilian "tech reps" (technical specialists) would come aboard to install upgrades to the equipment or make repairs. Rockville would deploy into the Atlantic and steam north and south towing these devices. Since the shore stations had our schedule and position they could calibrate their gear precisely. In her way Rockville made a significant contribution to the Cold War effort. Most of her crew, however, was more concerned with the demands of serving aboard a small ship.

I do not recall if duty aboard Rockville was considered to be "arduous sea duty" but it certainly was. I never worked harder in my life than on my tour abroad. I was assigned to Rockville before the Navy had established the Surface Warfare Officer School which served as post-graduate education for the junior officer and which vastly improved the effectiveness of newly commissioned surface officers. I had to learn my seamanship the old fashioned way, by on the job training.

Rockville carried a crew of fifty-two enlisted men and six officers. The Commanding Officer, a "mustang," (an enlisted sailor who advanced to a commissioned officer) was LT James Boyd. The

Executive Officer was a second tour Lieutenant Junior Grade (LT JG). There were four Ensigns plus me. Although I was junior, I made about a hundred dollars more a month than the other four because of my four years enlisted Navy Reserve time while attending the university. I always maxed out my pay grade about two years after each promotion because of my previous longevity, credited for pay purposes.

The day I walked aboard Rockville I was designated a Department Head (Supply), the Damage Control Assistant (DCA), the Main Propulsion Assistant (MPA), the Assistant Offline Cryptology Officer, and immediately began training for Officer of the Deck In-Port and Underway. The four Ensigns were very eager for me to qualify so they could convert from a four section watch to a five section watch. I don't believe I have ever been as challenged as I was during that initial tour in the Navy. There was no shortage of responsibility and hard work. There was a demanding period of adjustment to become a seaman from a landlubber. In heavy weather and in not-so-heavy weather Rockville was tossed about like a cork in the ocean. I was desperately sea sick for about a week. It took me about six weeks of experiencing other than calm weather to get over being sea sick. One advantage of this experience, however, was that I've never been sea sick again.

As Supply Officer I was a Department Head and responsible for all requisitions for the ship's fuel, repair parts, rations and other requirements like toilet paper. Not only did I have to quickly learn what it took to keep the ship supplied but I had to learn an extraordinarily complex Navy supply system. The Navy has a Supply Officer Corps which required successful completion of a six month supply school to learn the procedures, forms and paperwork. I learned it on-the-job. I had one individual, a Storekeeper Third Class (SK3) who worked for me. He was fairly knowledgeable and was a help to me in learning the initial procedures and requirements. Of course the Skipper was my overall instructor. He showed me very patiently how to send my first CASREP (casualty report) while at sea, an experience still vivid in my mind after all these years.

As the DCA I was responsible for the ship's Repair Parties, damage control in the event of a casualty, and for the weight and balance of the ship. I had to learn all of the ship's systems, including the fuel, hydraulic, high pressure air, low pressure air, fresh water, salt water and firefighting systems. I had to master knowledge of the water-tight integrity of the spaces which included the doors, hatches and bulkhead penetration (packing glands) of the systems. The DCA responsibility itself could be a 24 hour a day learning experience initially. I carry a lifelong respect for the sailors in any ship's Repair Party who have fought a casualty at sea. Other than close quarter combat, I can't picture anything more demanding or life threatening.

As the Main Propulsion Assistant, I spent many hours in the engine room. Rockville was powered by two twelve cylinder diesel engines. When I reported aboard, the senior Engineman was a First Class Petty Officer. After a few months he rotated ashore and was replaced by a thoroughly knowledgeable Chief Petty Officer who made the diesels hum like clockwork. I never did get used to the smell of diesel fumes in the engine room which only compounded my misery in heavy weather when I was seasick.

Not only was I a Department Head when I reported aboard but also a Division Officer. As a Division Officer I was solely responsible for the engine room crew. My Storekeeper would also muster with the engine room crew since there was only one of him. It was during this tour that I cut my teeth on the hard lessons of leading enlisted sailors. I was fortunate that I had the Chief as my leading petty officer. He was able to provide me with a valuable education in how to be a Division Officer, lessons that I took with me and used for the rest of my Navy career.

The most demanding of all responsibilities was that of ship handling as Officer of the Deck (OOD), Underway. I learned the basics at OCS but they were only the basics. I had to master Rules of the Road, navigation, including celestial and LORAN, (Long Range Radio Communications) radio, and deck seamanship.

I wasn't aboard long when I received my first assignment as Officer of the Deck to command the ship as we unberthed from the pier to stand out to sea. I would later receive the benefit of the Navy's excellent structured and systematic aviation training effort, but learning my duties as OOD aboard Rockville was strictly by OJT

11

(on-the-job-training). Again, my best instructor was the Old Man, the Skipper.

I served as Junior Officer of the Deck (JOOD) for six special sea and anchor details so I had a chance to witness the getting underway evolution, but I was still extremely nervous on that first occasion. I remember it well. We were scheduled to get underway from the pier at the Little Creek Amphibious Base. Fortunately, there were no other ships tied up ahead or behind us. It was a gray overcast day in January. There was a wind of about five knots. A group of wives were present on the pier together with representatives from the Type Commander along with the line handling party to see us get under way. I was on the bridge well before the Skipper and completed the engine and steering tests so I knew everything was ready. When the skipper took the bridge he immediately went to his chair.

"The Captain is on the bridge!" the Boatswain's Mate of the Watch (BOW) declared.

"Good Morning, Captain," I greeted as I saluted.

"Good morning," he replied returning my salute. "Mr. Sierras has the Conn."

"Ensign Sierras has the Conn," the BOW repeated logging that fact into the ship's journal.

"I have the Conn. Captain, request permission to get the ship underway."

"Make it so," he replied.

After the brow was cleared and the crane was out of the way, I began the evolution. I am writing this some thirty seven years after this but I believe I still recall it clearly enough to remember it.

"Advise the Engine Room to standby to answer all bells," I ordered the Lee Helm (the Engine Order Telegraph Operator).

"Engine Room reports ready to answer all bells, Sir!" he reported.

"Very well," I acknowledged.

"Single up all lines," I ordered.

After the deck crew and the line handlers had complied and reported, the Sound Powered Telephone Talker advised, "The First Lieutenant reports all lines singled up, Sir!"

"Very well. Take in lines one, three and four," I ordered.

After the order was executed, "lines One, Three and Four clear and stowed, Sir."

"Very well. Right five degrees rudder, port engine back one third, starboard engine ahead one third."

"Right five degrees rudder! The rudder is right five degrees, Sir," the Helmsman reported.

"Port engine back one third, starboard engine ahead one third!" the Engine Order Telegraph operator reported. "The Engine Room answers, port engine back one third, starboard engine ahead one third, Sir!"

"Very well. Rudder amidships! All engines stop. Take in line two!" I commanded.

"Rudder amidships, Sir! Rudder is amidships, Sir!" the Helmsman responded.

"All engines stop, Sir! Engine room answers all engines stop, Sir!"

As soon as line two cleared the pier, the BOW ordered "Shift Colors!" over the 1 MC (the ship wide announcing system). At this point, the Boatswain's Mates struck the Ensign on the fantail and the Union Jack on the bow and the signalmen on the signal bridge raised the Ensign on the mast to signal a ship under way.

"Signal underway and backing down!" I ordered, telling the BOW to sound one long blast to signal to other ships we were away from the pier under our own power (underway) and the three short blasts to signal that we had our engines in reverse.

The Rockville was clear and backing down smartly. I had to steer her to ensure she backed down in a straight line to clear the pier, and then turn her in the right direction to leave the harbor and head for the open sea through the opening of the harbor. I did this with rudder and engine commands. It is much easier to steer a twin screwed ship than one with a single screw. Rockville answered her rudder and engine commands smartly with little lag time for a ship.

"Left five degrees rudder, all engines back one third!" I commanded.

"Left five degrees rudder, rudder is left five degrees, Sir!"

"All engines back one third! Engine room responds all engines back one third, Sir!"

"Very well. Rudder amidships!"

"Rudder amidships! Rudder is amidships, Sir!"

"Very well. Port engine back one third, starboard engine ahead one third."

"Port engine back one third, starboard engine ahead one third! Engine room answers port engine back one third, starboard engine ahead one third, Sir!"

"Very well. Starboard engine stop."

"Starboard engine stop. Engine room responds starboard engine stop."

"Port engine ahead one third, Sir!"

"Very well, starboard engine ahead one third. Mark your head!"

"Starboard engine ahead one third! Engine room responds starboard engine ahead one third, all engines ahead one third, Sir!"

"Passing two six-zero degrees, Sir!"

"Very well, steady on course two-six-three." I would stay on this course until we cleared the piers, providing us room to steer to the west, then northwest into the channel, then through the channel out to sea.

As we passed the tower at the Type Command's Headquarters building, the signalmen there were flashing "cleared to proceed. Godspeed."

After our signalman dutifully reported the message they requested permission to answer, which I gave. The procedures for leaving port were highly structured although it was possible to receive last minute instructions in this manner.

The crew was well drilled and responded as the professionals they were. The Skipper sat in his chair and had not muttered one word, an indication from him that he was satisfied with the way I was handling things at this time.

I was still extremely nervous and keyed up but I noticed that this served to make my perceptions razor sharp and I was ready to take corrective action should the need arise. I found that this intensity would remain throughout my naval career and would serve me well.

My next problem was to maintain more than steerageway (the minimum speed a vessel needs to be moving in order for its rudder to effectively control its direction) yet not cause a wake that could damage ships tied up to the piers or cause an undue wake against the shore. I must have hesitated too long because the Skipper commanded, "Gene, take her to ten knots."

"Aye, aye, Sir!" I replied. "All engines ahead two thirds, right standard rudder, steady on course two-niner-five."

The course of 295-degrees was recommended to me by the Navigator, the Executive Officer, who served in that capacity during the Special Sea and Anchor Detail.

I needed to adjust the RPM of the screws by giving the order to the engine room to set and maintain a precise number of RPM. I cannot recall at this late date what those were, although I remember there was a matrix on the bridge available to the Conning Officer to use to fine tune the speed. I continued to maneuver the ship as we entered the channel and proceeded through the channel into the Atlantic Ocean where I steered a southerly course for the Caribbean Sea and its islands.

After I requested and received permission from the Skipper to secure the Special Sea and Anchor Detail and set the regular steaming watch, I did so and was relieved by Ensign Sam Dunn.

As the Skipper was leaving the bridge he smiled at me and said, "well done." Rockville was his first command at sea and I was his first boot-Ensign so he took a special interest in my professional training. I was relieved and happy to have survived my first experience as Conning officer. There would be many more, of course, but the first one always stayed with me.

Duty aboard Rockville at sea was a tremendous learning experience. While at sea I stood watches with the other ensigns in four section watch until I was qualified as OOD Underway, then we went to five section watches. The evening watch was a dogged watch (two-hour watch) to permit the crew to mess. Reveille was at 0600 hours with muster at 0800. Knock off ship's work was at 1600 hours. When not on watch or on duty I was busy learning my duties and practicing seamanship and navigation.

Rockville had only LORAN and celestial navigation to navigate by. On one occasion Rockville was about a thousand miles off the coast of Africa in the South Atlantic, well beyond the range of our

15

LORAN receiver. We had to rely solely on celestial navigation. With practice I became fairly proficient at star shots and sun lines. When our operating schedule permitted, the Skipper would set up man overboard drills and provide us with an opportunity to practice ship handling drills over and over again until we became proficient in that procedure as well.

Although never at sea for long periods because of our fuel limitations, the crew would settle into a routine which served to sharpen our skills and seamanship. Rockville took us to many ports in the Caribbean. During the winter months it seemed as if half the Canadian Navy was in those parts and we made many acquaintances not only with Canadian sailors but Canadian vacationers as well. I had an opportunity to meet and date more than one pretty Canadian girl. Some of the civilians, both Canadian and American, were highly skilled sailors in their own right, crewing and sailing yachts and sailing vessels of all sizes and descriptions. Because of her size Rockville avoided heavy weather at all cost. Whenever there was a hurricane or tropical storm forecast to be anywhere near us we high-tailed it in the other direction to ensure we avoided it by at least two hundred miles.

I remember those days as hard work but idyllic. In the Caribbean, the ship went to tropical hours which meant the day began at 0600 but we knocked off ship's work at 1300 leaving plenty of time in the afternoon to go sightseeing or otherwise enjoying the islands.

By the time fall of 1965 arrived in the Caribbean I was proficient at conning the ship in an out of port. It was still an extremely demanding task for me, however, one that required my total concentration and effort. I had an opportunity to conn the ship for a repositioning either in late summer or early fall of 1965. It wasn't too long before our departure from the Caribbean for the cold waters of the North Atlantic when Rockville found herself tied up at the pier at Naval Station San Juan, Puerto Rico. We were tied port-side-to behind a fleet tug and in front of a fleet oiler. We were tied up at the innermost pier of a two pier facility so there was a second pier to our starboard about fifty yards away. Again, there was a pier side party to watch us maneuver out of the way so that the fleet tug in front of us could get underway for an assignment. I had the conn. Fortunately, there was a breeze of 5-to-10-knots blowing 90-degrees against the ship from starboard to port. After maneuvering on the number-2 line as the spring-line, I took in all lines, backed Rockville smartly between the fleet oiler and the pier to the starboard, cleared the area until the fleet tug backed down and cleared the area on its mission. I then conned Rockville back into the slip to the pier side location which had recently been vacated by the tug. I had to maneuver smartly to prevent the starboard wind from moving us too close to the oiler. Correctly gauging my position, I stopped all engines, backed down both engines until all forward progress had stopped, and let the wind move us exactly into the correct position for mooring. All lines were heaved-out and secured, the brow was repositioned, and we secured from the Special Sea and Anchor detail. The Skipper nodded his head towards me as he left the bridge to join the pier side party, not saying a word. The expression on his face, however, let me know he was pleased with my performance. No one else spoke a word. I realized then that praise was the absence of criticism. As a professional naval officer I was only expected to do my job competently.

In October of 1965 Rockville was ordered to depart San Juan, Puerto Rico to complete a mission in the North Atlantic after which we were scheduled for two port calls in Nova Scotia, one in Halifax and one in Sydney.

By this time I was proficient in my OOD duties even if I didn't qualify as an "Old Salt." I previously submitted a letter requesting application into the NFO (Naval Flight Officer) program and was scheduled for a battery of tests when we returned to Norfolk. The Skipper gave me a favorable recommendation on my request. He said he was a little disappointed that I decided not to make the surface Navy my career but understood my desire to fly. The United States' involvement in Vietnam was becoming more widely reported in the media so it looked as if there would be a greater demand for Navy personnel to serve in that theater. Some of the officers aboard considered requesting duty as Swift Boat skippers, a billet which was slotted for a LT JG with ship handling and boat experience. We all had that, including taking our turns as boat officer when we put the ship's Boston Whaler into the water.

It was with a little sadness but high expectations I experienced as I stood on the bridge as Rockville stood out to sea from San Juan Harbor.

After a period of some seven days Rockville completed her North Atlantic mission. We reeled in the "fish" and stowed it as we plotted our course for Halifax, Nova Scotia. We received steady reports of gale warnings between us and Nova Scotia but the Skipper wasn't about to request permission to divert from our assignment so we pressed on in ever worsening weather.

The officers received orders from the Skipper to rig for heavy weather. I thought I had experienced heavy weather in our journey through the Cape Hatteras area but the Old Man assured me that I did not yet experience heavy weather. He went over with me detailed procedures for securing for heavy seas. I experienced Rockville heaving, yawing, pitching, and rolling. I saw and heard dishes in the wardroom and crew's mess go sailing off the table to crash on the deck when the ship took what I considered to be heavy rolls. But I had absolute faith in the Old Man. He had been going to sea for over twenty years and he was always correct in his predictions. I spent a considerable amount of time with my leading petty officers and crew ensuring that everything possible was secured and tied down. I read the ship's Heavy Weather Bill (a set of procedures to follow when hazardous weather is predicted, such as a hurricane or major storm.) over and over until I memorized it. It was a good thing I did. Rockville steamed into a full gale in the North Atlantic. The weather was cold but not cold enough to freeze sea water on deck or she would have suffered extremely dangerous conditions. Prior to encountering heavy weather the Skipper asked me for my recommendation on ballasting the fuel tanks. It was quite a while since I plotted the ship's righting arm moment so I was careful and worked out our stability profile several times until I was absolutely sure it was correct. I calculated that with our current fuel load our stability was such that the righting moment fell into the area in which it was recommended that the tanks be ballasted to lower the center of gravity to increase the righting moment. It was my responsibility as the DCA to recommend to the Commanding Officer that we ballast the tanks. This action would require that Rockville enter into a shipyard to clean the fuel tanks contaminated with the sea water. The Skipper looked at my computations very carefully. He didn't speak for what I considered to be quite a lengthy period of time. Finally, he looked up at me and said, "Mr. Sierras (junior officers in the Navy were addressed as "Mr."), I agree with your calculations and with your recommendations. However, I cannot take on seawater at this point because it would require a lengthy yard period to purge the tanks. I will order that the ship be kept into the seas at all times. We will be okay." He did, however, order the Navigator to ensure my recommendation and his decision were entered into the ship's journal.

It wasn't until Rockville was in the full gale with the freezing weather and gale force winds that I realized how real the possibility of seawater freezing on deck could be. If this happened it would decrease the stability of the ship to the extent that she would be in imminent danger of broaching. The Skipper would have to send crews out onto the weather decks in gale conditions to chip away the ice. Even if this measure were successful the chances were likely that several of the crew would be lost at sea. However, measured against the risk of losing the entire ship it would have been necessary to do it. With the advantage of hindsight, the Skipper made the correct decision. If I were in the same circumstance, I would have ballasted the tanks with seawater and taken the consequences.

Over the years many of the memories of my tour on Rockville have faded. Not the memory of her at sea in the gale. Even over the span of 37 years I can vividly recall what it was like standing watch on the bridge listening to the winds whipping through the stays with such force that it caused a continuous howling or moaning sound. The Rockville's bridge was an open one. The front and sides were fitted with glass windshields. The overhead was tightly lashed canvas. Therefore, people on the bridge were exposed to the wind and cold if not rain. The canvas kept most of the green water crashing over the bow from soaking us. Green water was crashing over the bridge! A little water could get through in the open spaces between the canvas lashings and the windscreen. The sound of the sea was continuous. I remember standing watch as OOD. Only the phone talker and I were on the bridge. Everyone else stood watch in the wheelhouse to keep them out of the elements. I remember keeping the ship headed into the seas. Rockville would ride up the swell until at the crest I could look down into the trough, a veritable chasm, a literal chasm between us and the next giant wave of water. Then she would ride down the sea until we were in the trough. At this point I could look up, craning my neck to do so, gazing in wonder at this giant wave of water, easily thirty feet above me at the crest! At any time, had Rockville placed the seas at her beam, we would have broached, taking all hands with her.

We could not light the galley fires so the crew was served sandwiches and "bug juice" (an endearing name for a colored sweetened soft drink) for our entire sojourn through the gale. The crew could not work, only stand critical watches and stay in their bunks or sit hanging on with both hands to whatever they sat on. To attempt to do anything else meant constantly fighting to prevent being tossed from one side of the ship to the other. We set modified general quarters to ensure as many doors and hatches were dogged as possible in the event of flooding.

About the fifth day we began to experience a lessening of the force. Gradually the wind began to reduce in intensity and the seas began to decrease. I remember standing the second dog watch on the fifth day when my Second Class cook brought my phone talker and me a freshly baked loaf of bread. We all lost a few pounds by then from the steady diet of sandwiches. The smell and taste of that freshly baked bread is still vivid in my memory. At that particular time, the three of us shared a camaraderie that comes only from sharing an intense, demanding experience. After I was relieved I went down and ate in the crew's mess. It was my responsibility to eat in the crew's mess periodically as the Supply Officer to ensure the quality was satisfactory. Since our wardroom was too small to have its own galley the officers ate the same food as the crew. It was the opportunity to sit down with the crew and swap stories about our experiences that was the pleasure of sharing a meal with them.

Rockville rode out the storm. She steamed through the North Atlantic on a much more even keel now as the seas quieted and the wind abated. The next morning Rockville was to be at the entrance to the channel into Halifax Harbor at first light. I was scheduled for the mid-watch (midnight to 0400) so I turned in right after the Eight O'clock Reports. (A daily report that Department Heads were required to make to the XO at 2000-hours. My report included the fact that the galley fires were out.)

The Messenger of the Watch awakened me at 2330 hours from a dead sleep, the first restful sleep I had since Rockville entered into the gale. I quickly dressed then stopped by the mess decks for a fresh cup of coffee. I reported to the bridge a little earlier than the relief time of 2345-hours to let my eyes dark-adapt, to review the Captain's Night Orders, and to look at the radar repeater on the bridge. I could see that we were off the coast of Nova Scotia. I was relieving recently promoted LT JG Brad Wesley, an Ivy League graduate who had been in the Navy a full eighteen months.

The Captain's Night Orders directed that Rockville run an oval race track pattern off the coast and be in position at the mouth of the channel at first light so we could begin our approach as early as possible. The Standing Night Orders required that the Skipper be notified anytime any vessel was on a course that would bring her to a CPA (closest point of approach) of 8,000 yards, or four miles, or closer. The OOD would plot the course using maneuvering board and radar, call the Skipper on the sound powered phone directly to his at-sea cabin, then make a recommendation on what action to take.

After I had completed my qualification the Skipper would come to the bridge anytime I called him at night with a CPA of an approaching vessel that was 8,000 yards or closer. After I was qualified for two months he quit doing that unless the situation was such that a potential problem could develop. The Skipper, like the entire crew, was exhausted from riding out the gale. LT JG Wesley was himself exhausted and told me that he had experienced a considerable amount of difficulty in staying awake. He also informed me that some of the ships bottled up in Halifax Harbor during the storm were now beginning to put out to sea. Two of the ships approached Rockville with a CPA of 8,000 yards or closer. The Skipper acknowledged Brad's first call but didn't answer the second call.

Brad completed his briefing by advising me that directly to our west, several thousand yards off the coast clearly indicated on the radar scope, was a line of shoals that Rockville must steer clear. The shoals would always be to our west about 4,000 yards during the inshore portion of our racetrack pattern. He admonished me to exercise care during my watch as I relieved him and he struck below to collapse into his bunk.

Here I was on that cold October night in the North Atlantic. My watch crew consisted of the Quartermaster of the Watch (QOW), the Helmsman and Lee Helmsman in the wheelhouse below the bridge, the Messenger of the Watch (MOW), the Phone Talker, and two Signalmen on the signal bridge. The Engineer of the Watch (EOW) and his talker were in the engine room. The rest of the crew of Rockville was sleeping in an exhausted state after riding out the storm. I had been on active duty in the Navy for fourteen months, ten of those months as a commissioned officer aboard Rockville, and eight as a qualified OOD. I was sobered by my responsibilities.

I didn't have much time to reflect on my situation, however. At least ten ships in Halifax Harbor decided to put to sea that night. Each stood out from Halifax in the channel and depending on Rockville's position in her race track pattern would approach well within the 8,000 yard CPA requiring that I call the Skipper to advise him. Each ship would also render honors to an American Man-of-war with their signal lamps requiring a response from Rockville. Things became busy almost immediately. The first two ships passed near Rockville with a CPA of 5,000 yards when we were at the northwest extreme of our race track pattern. I dutifully plotted their course and CPA using radar and maneuvering board then called the Skipper on the sound powered telephone. The first time I called I had to make four attempts at turning the crank to activate the call alarm at the Skipper's phone before he answered. I advised him of the required information and my recommendation which he acknowledged with an incoherent mumble.

The second attempt was fruitless so I dispatched the Messenger to knock at the door of his At-Sea cabin. The MOW reported back that there was no answer and he believed he could hear the Skipper snoring. From that point on, although I dutifully attempted to contact the skipper for the next dozen or so vessels that approached Rockville with a CPA of 8,000 yards or less, I was on my own. The Skipper was too exhausted to answer. I did instruct the Quartermaster to enter each incident into the ship's journal. I was responsible for the safety of Rockville and her crew. I kept station by piloting and LORAN ensuring that we never approached less than 4,000 yards to the shoal rocks on our west, and adjusting our course to ensure that Rockville would be in position to be at the mouth of the channel at First Light. The four-hour watch went by quickly since I was extremely busy. My watch team functioned perfectly. The signalmen would report the content of each ship's signal lamp message and promptly relay my response. Most ships continued on a southwesterly course after leaving the channel for a few miles which made my problem easier, but two or three turned immediately to the south which caused me to plot CPAs less than 2,000 yards abeam. I changed course and speed to avoid them then to correct back to course.

When I was relieved by LT JG John Reynolds, the senior JG and the Senior Watch Officer, I received kudos for a job well done. By that time, the number of ships leaving port had been reduced (I believe my crew and I counted twelve that departed on our watch). He told me to strike below and get some sleep because I was due back on the bridge in less than two hours for the Special Sea and Anchor Detail. I was to be the JOOD and John would be the Conning Officer taking her into berth next to a Canadian destroyer which would be our host for our port visit. Other than the brief kudo from John no one ever mentioned anything about my watch. I took this as an indicator that I had the full trust of the Skipper and my peers and no less would be expected of me in the future. I had a smile on my fact as I struck below and crawled into my rack. Within seconds I was asleep.

USS Rockville (EPCER851) in her World War II configuration

CHAPTER THREE

Jinking Bogey

"THE F-4 PHANTOM II IS A TWO-PLACE (TANDEM) SUPERSONIC, LONG-range, all-weather fighter built by McDonnell Douglas Corporation. The aircraft is designed for intermediate and long range high altitude interceptions using missiles as the principal armament and for intermediate or long range attack missions to deliver airborne weapons/ stores. The aircraft is powered by two single rotor, axial flow, variable stator turbo-jets J79-GE-8 or J79-GE-10 engines with afterburner."

So begins the DESCRIPTION paragraph in the Navy's NATOPS Flight Manual. NATOPS stands for Naval Air Training and Operating Procedures Standardization Program. The Phantom was designed in the mid 1950 period to provide the Navy with a high-altitude, high-Mach all-weather interceptor against high-altitude long-range Soviet strike-aircraft. With the Phantom II the Navy for the first time had a true over-the-horizon all-weather interceptor that could seek out and destroy an airborne threat to the fleet before that threat could get into launch range. Working with Airborne Early Warning (AEW) aircraft like the E1 Tracer, the Navy expanded its over the horizon detection and intercept capability while operating in blue water or deep at sea. Under the old Navy nomenclature, the E1 Tracer, was designated "WF" and affectionately dubbed the "Willy Fudd". Since it was based on the "S2" aircraft it later became known as the "Stoof with a Roof". It was replaced by the advanced and highly capable "E2 Hawkeye" Airborne Early Warning aircraft. I saw the "Stoofs" operating off many aircraft carriers both during my reserve active duty for training periods and later flying in the Phantom. It was with the Hawkeye that the Phantom became fully capable of seeking out and destroying an airborne enemy against the fleet in all weather conditions day or night.

The planners of that day believed that the days of the typical "dogfight," or close in air engagements between maneuvering fighters, were over and that the future held out the probability of Soviet high altitude long-range attacks against a fleet operating in blue water, or deep at sea. They did not envision the Phantom would engage Soviet built MiG aircraft in just such "dog fighting" over North Vietnam. (The correct Navy term for dog fighting is Air Combat Maneuvering, or ACM.) Therefore, the Phantom was not provided with an internal cannon, although later the Navy Phantoms could be fitted with the MK-4 gun pod in the centerline station.

Air Force Phantoms were later provided an internal cannon with the advent of the F-4E. However, because of the swept wing configuration, the Phantom is at a disadvantage against a more highly maneuverable, tighter turning fighter. Navy aircrews learned how to exploit the Phantom's strengths while minimizing its weaknesses by the use of superior tactics and incessant training.

To the best of my knowledge the Phantom never fired a shot in anger against Soviet aircraft attacking a fleet at sea. That didn't mean that aircrews didn't constantly practice for that mission, however. I can remember countless training flights practicing all weather intercepts against airborne threats.

One of those missions was that of a "jinking bogey." A "bogey" is a term from the ACP-165 (Allied Communications Publication) which provides definitions for operational brevity words used in air combat. It lists over one hundred terms alphabetically from A to Z with short definitions for an unknown aircraft. A bogey becomes a "bandit" when it is positively identified as a hostile aircraft. Identification can be either visual or electronic. Obviously, an aircraft, or flight of aircraft, attacking the fleet, would not attempt to fly straight and level, all other considerations being equal. Such a constant heading and constant air speed would solve the fire control solution for the Phantom. Therefore, an attack aircraft would not fly at a constant heading, constant altitude, and/or constant speed, unless fuel constraints required it to do so. At extended ranges from the Soviet homeland, however, fuel constraints would limit attacking aircraft. But it would be in the Soviet aircrew's best interest to change those factors as much as possible. An aircraft flying such a changing flight path is termed a "jinking bogey."

Navy aircrews start with the basic intercept using the APQ-72 pulse radar or the AWG-10 Pulse Doppler radar flying as a single aircraft against another single aircraft. The complexity of the intercept progresses until multiple aircraft intercept multiple aircraft using the "jinking bogey" flight profile. The only constraints are that the attacking aircraft must realistically fly a pattern that would permit them to strike the target which the interceptor is defending.

One of my favorite training missions was the jinking bogey intercept at night against a single dissimilar aircraft such as a Navy EA3 Sky Warrior. The Sky Warrior started out its life as an aircraft carrier-based long range attack bomber. By the time I reached the fleet in the mid to late sixties it lost that mission due to the high threat environment over land. Navy attack aircraft like the A4 Sky Hawk, the all-weather A6 Intruder, and the A7 Corsair II, as well as the versatile Phantom, had assumed that role. The Sky Warrior was given the carrier borne electronic warfare mission and the tanking mission (any tanker is near and dear to Phantom aircrews).

But it was still a good platform, typically with a crew of three, a pilot, a navigator, and an electronic warfare officer. With a full load of fuel it could fulfill the jinking bogey role. It also could use electronic countermeasures against the Phantom such as chaff, jamming, and electronic deception which could fool the Phantom's fire control system by gradually delaying the returning pulse to throw off the antenna's ability to automatically track the target. To conclude a successful intercept Phantom aircrews had to use all the options provided by the Phantom's system including Home-On-Jam, Manual Track, and narrow scan.

I recall one night mission which was typical. I was assigned to Fighter Squadron 84 (VF 84) in 1974. Normally we would have deployed with our sister squadron aboard the USS Roosevelt (CVA 42), but this was the year that the Navy wanted to experiment with placing one expanded fighter squadron aboard a carrier instead of two. The Navy recently lost its anti-submarine aircraft carriers and was consolidating both the anti-submarine (CVS) Air Wing and the attack carrier (CVA) Air wing, redesignating the Roosevelt a CV. There just wasn't enough room with all the additional aircraft aboard the tired old carrier for two fully manned fighter squadrons. As a result, some aircrews and aircraft were transferred temporarily to our sister squadron and VF 84 remained ashore during that deployment. There were two advantages for those of us who remained. We went to a four day work week (the only time in my life I ever was lucky enough to experience that) and we were able to fly a great many training missions. We also made several "hot pad" deployments to Key West. In those days, the United States was flying reconnaissance missions over Cuba. Policy required that whenever a recon bird was over Cuba the US had to have armed and ready fighters on 5-minute alert status able to become airborne within five minutes to fend off enemy fighters should the recon aircraft be threatened. The Navy and the Air Force would swap ready fighter status every two weeks. The Air Force maintained their alert birds at Homestead Air Force Base and the Navy kept their fighters at Naval Air Station Key West.

A result of our remaining ashore, we were able to request and receive assets that normally would be difficult to schedule. One of these assets was the EA3 (affectionately known as the "electronic whale", to differentiate it from the A3, or regular old "whale"). I requested and been assigned a training air intercept mission against the EA3 off the coast of Virginia in March of 1974. The air/sea temperature allowed us the luxury of not wearing the exposure suit. The mission was to be a night flight. I was scheduled to fly with my pilot, LT John Reynolds, a recently arrived and promoted officer who had come to VF-84 from the replacement squadron, VF-101. The EA3 crew was part of a detachment stationed out of Naval Air Station (NAS) Norfolk, their main squadron being stationed at NAS Jacksonville in Florida. John and I traveled to their ready room at NAS Norfolk for a crew to crew briefing, covering such details as launch time, frequencies, stations, emergency procedures, divert procedures and a myriad of other details involved in a typical mission briefing.

The pilot of the EA3 was LCDR William Croft, the Navigator/ Bombardier was LT Sean Johnson, and the Electronic Warfare Officer (EWO) was LT Bradley Cousins, an LDO. (LDO, Limited Duty Officer, typically an ex-enlisted individual who had been commissioned as an officer because of his special expertise and who worked strictly in his specialty. LDOs were typically very skilled and typically deeply knowledgeable in their specialty.) Bradley had more time in the Navy than any of us although he was the junior officer in rank. It didn't take me long to discern that Bradley knew his system inside and out. As an enlisted man he had attended the Navy's highly technical schools to learn how to repair the system. As a commissioned officer he was responsible for the entire squadron's maintenance effort of the system. And as an EWO he had attended the Navy's supremely excellent flight officer schools in his warfare specialty. He also had an extensive amount of airborne experience in the system and had actually used his system against Soviet aircrews both in the Mediterranean and in the Pacific theaters. He had also "spoofed" many a Phantom aircrew, humiliating more than one while providing them excellent experience in intercepting an aircraft in an electronic warfare environment. To quote an old Navy saying, "you can't buy training like that."

I eagerly looked forward to meeting the AE 3 as John and I went through our briefing and pre-flight inspection. We launched at 1900-hours from NAS Oceana. After the Standard Instrument Departure (SID) we changed frequencies to our tactical air controller stationed at Dam Neck, Virginia, just south of NAS Oceana. All my systems checks were good and I had a good operating radar. We were vectored to the exercise area and waited for the EA 3 to check in, which it did right on time. Our first intercept began immediately after the Sky Warrior reported on station and ready.

The first intercept began with a forty-five mile separation. Altitude was to be between five-thousand and thirty-thousand feet. The EA3 was north and we were south. It could vary its heading, air speed and altitude as it desired, keeping with the target strike parameters it would have to use in the real world if it were attacking our fleet. The mission could last as long as we desired so there were no fuel constraints. At a certain fuel state, we would terminate the mission and return to base so the EA3 had more than ample fuel.

The voice of the air controller came over the radio, "Eagle Two-Zero-Two, vector south, set airspeed and Angels as desired." (Angels is the ACP-165 code for altitude.)

"Showtime Six-Zero-Two (our call sign) vector three-five-zero (degrees) for bogey, elevator (climb or descend to) Angels-15. Your bogey is three-five-zero, forty-five miles."

John advised me when we were steady on magnetic heading 350-degrees, that we were at 15-thousand feet, and our air speed was 350-knots Calibrated Airspeed. (The speed of an aircraft as indicated on its airspeed indicator, corrected for any errors caused by the instrument's position or installation.)

I selected fifty-mile range display on the APQ72 radar. We were flying the F4N. (The F4N was the F4B reworked to extend its airframe life. It had the basic configuration as the original F4B, with updated electronics.)

I originally selected level antenna, one bar scan, but soon realized the EA3 was not at our altitude. I figured he had been climbing since departure to thirty thousand feet and would convert that altitude to air speed during our flight. I was correct. I elevated the antenna slightly and picked him up at 43 miles, at 30,000 feet. I did not attempt lock-on. To do so, I would tell Bradley, the EWO, that I had a full systems lock which I didn't desire to do quite yet. (Full system lock provides automatic antenna tracking and display of the fire control solution on both the front and rear radar scopes.)

"Showtime Six-Zero-Two, contact three-five-zero degrees, forty-three miles," I radioed our GCI (ground control intercept) controller.

To John I said, "he's dead ahead, forty-three miles, thirty-thousand feet."

"That's your bogey, Punch," (ACP 165 codeword for your bogey is in range and you should be able to take control of the intercept) radioed the controller.

"I'm not going to take a "Judy" yet. I'm going to wait for a few more miles before doing so. I want him to initiate countermeasures while we're still in search (mode)," I told John.

"Roger that," John responded, "he sure makes a nice target." "That wily EWO just punched out a bundle of chaff. That makes the target appear so big. Watch me as I relocate him," I told John.

I gradually lowered the antenna and reacquired the EA3. This time he was about five thousand feet lower and descending and therefore, accelerating. If I had attained full systems lock, the chaff would have transferred our automatic tracking from the aircraft to the bundle of chaff, then seconds later would have broken lock (hopefully, sometimes the chaff would hold lock for several minutes in "memory mode." More than once I tracked a bundle of chaff mistakenly.)

I located him 15-degrees left of our nose or at 345-degrees magnetic.

"Port to three-two-five-degrees. He's varied his heading to about two-one-zero-degrees. He's still descending and accelerating," I told John. "In a few seconds I'll lock him up to see what he'll do next."

"Your bogey is three-three-five-degrees, thirty-five miles, Punch," GCI radioed.

"Showtime Six-Zero-Two, contact three-three-zero degrees, thirty-two miles," I responded.

"That's your bogey, Punch," GCI radioed back.

"Showtime Six-Zero-Two, Judy, out," I radioed, advising GCI that I was taking control of the intercept and would not require further calls.

"Look at that trail of chaff!" John said over the intercom system (ICS, the inter-cockpit communications system).

"Yes. Port to three-one-zero. Contact will be on the nose at thirty-miles. He's dropping chaff because we haven't locked him up yet. He's making us work," I explained to John.

At that time, the AE3 was at about our altitude, 15,000 feet, doing about 450-knots CAS, converting its altitude to speed. We had about 40-degrees of left target aspect, or TA. (Target Aspect is the bearing that the target would see us relative to his nose. In this case, he would see us 40 degrees left of his nose, although we saw him dead ahead, or on our nose. TA is measured from the nose, port or starboard to the tail of the aircraft, or 40-degrees left.)

We were in a beam run which means we could not obtain a firing position for our AIM7 Sparrow missile. At this point, we would either have to increase our speed and turn further port to put him at about

40-degrees right of our nose to "cut him off at the pass", or increase speed. We could also run a rear quarter attack which would give us back our Sparrow option, but, even better, would give us the AIM9D, Sidewinder, option. However, as I explained to John, he would have to change course towards us eventually to obtain an attack solution of his target, which we were defending.

"Port to two-niner-zero degrees. When steady, he'll be about twenty-degrees right, slightly lower, and I estimate about four-fifty knots. I'm going to lock him up," I told John.

"Lock up, twenty-degrees right, inside collision bearing, twenty-five miles, Overtake nine-hundred knots." (Overtake is the relative closing velocity between the interceptor and its target.)

The attack display with the AIM7 fire control solution was on both radar scopes so John could see it as well. The attack display includes a "steering dot," which when centered, would put the Phantom on collision bearing with the Sky Warrior. However, I anticipated a change in heading with a more reduced target aspect. It is conceivable that if we maneuvered to obtain an AIM7 shot at the Whale's current heading and he changed course towards we could cross his flight path and be out of position.

"John, look at the display," I said. The steering dot is slowly moving right and so is the blip. He's changing course more towards us. The Overtake is also increasing. It's nine-hundred-fifty knots. He is continuing to descend.

"Starboard to three-one-zero degrees, go down five-thousand, level at ten-thousand, set four hundred knots," I told John.

The bogey was turning left, beyond a heading of 180 degrees according to the drift and the movement of the steering dot and still descending according to the lowering elevation strobe on the attack display. By descending five thousand feet we could convert some of our altitude to air speed.

When we steadied at 310-degrees, the bogey was 30-degrees left and holding at collision bearing. The steering dot was centered which meant we were on a collision course of 120 degrees track crossing angle. The bogey now saw us 30-degrees right of his nose, or we had 30 degrees of right-target aspect. The range was now seventeen miles and the overtake was close to one thousand knots. The maximum range marker on the azimuth display indicated about 12-miles. At this point, I expected the steering dot to move to the left towards the target in a "transition mode" to steer the Phantom towards the optimum firing angle. At the maximum range of twelve miles, the steering circle, in which the steering dot was to be centered would start to expand, reaching maximum diameter at the heart of the firing envelope which would be about eight miles, giving the AIM7 its maximum probability of a kill.

The elevation strobe continued to lower, indicating that the AE3 was continuing its descent.

"Go down five thousand, level at five-thousand, set four-fifty," I commanded.

John quickly started the descent. Both of us were constantly monitoring the flight instruments as well as the radar scopes. I would read off airspeed and altitudes as they changed in a monotone voice to serve as a backup for John as he kept his scan working.

"Thirty-degrees left, fourteen-miles, overtake twelve-hundred knots, level. Bogey is five thousand feet. We are at five thousand feet," I advised John.

As the bogey approached twelve miles the dot transitioned to the left requiring a turn to the left to be in position to fire the AIM7 (the missile flies much faster than the Phantom, requiring less lead). At this time, the azimuth strobe turned an intense bright green indicating that the Sky Warrior was jamming us with a frequency similar to that of our radar causing us to lose range information. I selected HOJ (home on jam). The fire control computer was now tracking the range based in memory based on the last known relative closure. Had we fired an AIM7 at this point, the missile would have had to use its "Fuse On Jam" capability because it had no real time range information, only that provided by the computer in memory.

By the time the range strobe had closed to optimum range of about 8-miles I did not believe we could make a successful AIM7 shot. With the lack of range information and what I believed to be the electronic deception by the way the azimuth strobe was moving, I elected to convert to a rear quarter shot.

"Port hard!" I commanded. "He's jamming and deceiving. We're going for the Sidewinder."

John wrapped the aircraft into a 45-degree angle of bank and I could hear the engine respond to the advancing throttle position.

"Eagle-Two-Zero-Two, Showtime, request lights out for training," I radioed. I wanted to complete the intercept completely on radar with no visual cues. We would keep our lights on for flight safety.

"Roger, Showtime", Eagle responded.

"I'm breaking lock," I told John. "We'll complete this intercept in search. Reverse!"

John snapped the aircraft into a starboard 45-degree angle of bank.

"Forty-five-degrees right, five-miles, level at five thousand," I advised John. "He's dropping chaff again."

The chaff was obvious on the radar display in ten mile range. The target was a much smaller blip than the large chaff returns.

I felt the tightening of my g-suit as we pulled about four "gs" acceleration.

"Ease," I commanded and John eased on the stick gradually reducing our angle of bank.

'Hold," I commanded to John as we rolled to about a thirty degree angle of bank. We were approaching the rear of the target passing 120 degrees magnetic heading.

"Throttle back, set four hundred, steady on one-six-zero"

We continued our turn until heading 160 degrees magnetic, which was the bogey's current heading. He was dead ahead 1.5 miles, level. We were closing with about a relative closure of fifty knots.

"Go down one thousand, level at four thousand," I commanded. "Switch heat" (select the AIM 9D, Sidewinder missile).

John selected the AIM9 missile and we could hear the growl of the missile seeker head.

"Good growl!" John exclaimed.

"Bogey is at 1 mile, dead ahead, one thousand feet high, in range," I advised.

"Fox 2!" John radioed over the air. The growl of the Sidewinder's seeker head was so loud that I asked him to turn the volume down a little.

"Eagle, request lights on," I radioed.

When the AE3 responded, he was right on the nose, slightly high, one mile range, in the heart of the missile firing envelope with an overtake of about fifty knots.

"Good job, Showtime!" The AE3 radioed.

"Thanks, Eagle. Let's do it again!"

"Ruthless Ruth, request separation for another run," I radioed GCI.

"Roger, Showtime. Eagle Two-Oh-Two vector two-seven-zero-degrees for separation. Showtime Six-Oh-Two, vector zero-nine-zero degrees for separation."

"Roger, right to two-seven-zero," Eagle returned.

"Roger, left to zero-niner-zero," I replied.

I thought to myself, "And to think, I'm getting paid for this!"

CHAPTER FOUR

Geometry

THE PHANTOM IS AN ALL-WEATHER INTERCEPTOR, AMONG ITS OTHER capabilities. It is a point interceptor, unlike the F14 Tomcat, which has the capability to track multiple targets at the same time and fire multiple missiles at multiple targets. The Phantom's aircrew has a fire control computer aboard to develop and display an attack solution. The aircrew has to master the basics of intercept geometry in order to successfully prosecute an attack under real world conditions.

The Radar Intercept Officer (RIO) begins training in airborne intercept attack initially at Naval Air Technical Training Center Glynco (NATTC Glynco) which was located at Naval Air Station (NAS) Glynco, Georgia, located just outside the town of Brunswick, Georgia. I believe it was in the early 70's when Training Squadron Eighty Six (VT 86) was commissioned at NAS Pensacola, and combined all NFO training, but when I went through, training was at Glynco. I learned my airborne training in the T-39 Sabreliner, which incidentally, is still flying with VT 86. Two recently (May 2002) went down and were lost with all aircrew in the Gulf of Mexico south of NAS Pensacola. The Sabreliner had the same wing as the F 86 Sabre.

In those days, the Sabreliner was equipped with the APQ 94 radar, which was the Airborne Intercept (AI) radar used in the F8 Crusader. The APQ 72 radar used in the F4B and F4N was a quantum leap in capability over the APQ 94, and the AWG 10 radar used in the F4J and F4S was a quantum leap in capability over the APQ 72. The fact remained that unless the aircrew mastered basic intercept geometry they would never successfully fight the Phantom to its full capability in the interceptor mission.

I suspect the original intercept geometry instruction was conceived and written by engineers. Thankfully, aircrew instructors eventually improved it to the extremely basic fundamentals necessary to grasp and use it under real world conditions. I was tasked to write and distribute a student hand out guide when I was an instructor in VF101, the east coast RAG. (Replacement Air Group, from an earlier era. Now a squadron, it was still referred to as the "RAG.") I am recreating the essentials of that guide from memory about twenty-years later, a tribute to the thoroughness and professionalism of my instructors, both in basic, intermediate, and advanced training.

To begin with the basics, the following conditions are assumed:

Both aircraft, the "bogey" and the interceptor, are at the same speed;

The "bogey" aircraft will maintain a constant heading.

Picture an overhead or "plan" view of the two aircraft, with sixty mile separation. The bogey is heading 180-degrees; the interceptor is heading 360-degrees.

The interceptor would have to turn 180-degrees, from 360-to 180, in order to be on the same heading as the bogey. This is defined as the "Track Crossing Angle," or TCA.

If the bogey is "dead ahead," or on the interceptor's nose, bearing 360-degrees, when the distance closed to zero-range, and if the altitude were the same, the bogey and interceptor would collide with each other.

Therefore, "collision bearing" for a 180 degree Track Crossing Angle (180 TCA) is dead-ahead, or zero-degrees off the nose, or zero-degrees relative bearing. Relative bearing is defined as the number of degrees left or right of the interceptors extended flight path, or nose, that a target bears.

If the bogey were 5-degrees left of the interceptor's flight path, or 5-degrees left relative bearing, the bogey would not be on collision bearing but would drift as follows, relative to the interceptor's extended flight path, or nose:

37

At 60 miles separation, or range, the bogey is 5-degrees left;

At 30 miles range, the bogey is 10-degrees left;
At 15 miles range, the bogey is 20-degrees left;
At 7.5 miles range, the bogey is 40-degrees left;
At 3.75 miles range, the bogey is 80-degrees left;

As the two pass each other, the bogey will be abeam of the interceptor and will continue to increase degrees off collision bearing, or "angles off," until at some time in the future, at an extended range, the bogey will be almost 180-degrees off the tail.

The essential observation, or rule, to take from this example is that a bogey that is on collision bearing will not drift as range decreases (constant bearing, decreasing range, will always result in a collision if the altitude is equal); A corollary of that rule is: a bogey not on collision bearing will drift.

A bogey not on collision bearing will drift at a rate that will double its degrees off collision bearing as the range between the two aircraft halves (as shown in the example above, a 180 TCA, the bogey 5 degrees left). The Phantom's AI radar is a segment of a planned position indicator (PPI). A PPI is a 360-degree radar sweep.

The Phantom's AI radar takes a 60-degree segment, and expands the bottom sweep so that the origin of the sweep is not a point but is spread out over the width of the 60-degree scope. This results in not only a more useable scope at distances less than 5-miles, but an increased, more noticeable drift rate at close ranges.

In the following examples, the bogey will be heading 180-degrees:

The interceptor is heading 350-degrees. The TCA is 170-degrees (the interceptor would have to turn 170-degrees from a heading of 350 degrees to parallel the bogeys' 180-degree heading: the direction that the bogey's flight path takes relative to the interceptor's flight path, describes the direction of the TCA. In this example, the geometry is a 170 right TCA, or the bogey is flying from the interceptor's right to his left. The shortest direction of turn is left to 180-degrees: The shortest number of degrees to turn defines the TCA: of course, the interceptor could turn the opposite direction, or 190-degrees, but that option is discarded for numerous reasons).

For two co-speed aircraft, the collision bearing for a 170 TCA, is 5-degrees relative bearing, or, in this case, 5-degrees-right of the interceptor's nose, on a magnetic bearing of 355-degrees. If the two aircraft were too close to zero range at the same altitude, they would collide and the bogey would be 5-degrees right of the interceptor's nose until collision.

The difference between the interceptor's heading and the reciprocal of the bogey's heading, 360-degrees, is 10-degrees. The interceptor would have to turn right 10-degrees to be on a heading of 360-degrees, which is the reciprocal of the bogey's heading of 180-degrees. This angle, the angle from the interceptor's heading to the bogey's reciprocal, is called the "Make Up Angle."

For co-speed aircraft, collision bearing is always half of the Make Up Angle. Or in the case of a 170-degree TCA, the Make Up Angle (MUA) is 10-degrees, and the collision bearing is one half the MUA, or 5-degrees.

The TCA and the MUA will always be equal to 180 degrees.

For a quick additional example, we'll make the bogey be on a different bogey heading of 210-degrees. The reciprocal of 210 degrees is 030-degrees. An interceptor heading 020-degrees would be on a 170-degree right TCA, and the collision bearing would be 5-degrees right, or a bearing of 025-degrees.

Return to the bogey heading of 180 degrees: If the interceptor is heading 040-degrees, the interceptor is on a 140-degree left TCA (the bogey is traveling from the interceptor's left to its right; the interceptor would have to turn right 140-degrees to parallel the bogey's heading) The MUA is 40 degrees-left, and collision bearing is 20-degrees left.

The Phantom's fire control computer uses this solution to place the interceptor on a collision bearing because that is the quickest way to close the bogey. However, at some point, either the fire control computer or the aircrew would have to make an adjustment on the intercept for a successful firing because the Sparrow missile flies much faster than the Phantom. Obviously, the aircraft would not need as much lead for the missile to collide with the bogey, so the fire control computer computes a different intercept geometry for the missile, which requires much less lead. However, it doesn't go from an aircraft intercept solution instantaneously to a missile fire solution, but does so gradually. This gradual re-computation from an intercept solution to a firing solution is to "transition the steering dot."

The APQ 72 would begin to transition the dot to achieve a firing solution at maximum computer range. If the aircrew would attempt to turn the aircraft to keep the dot centered, it would result in something less than the optimum firing solution so aircrews would determine at what range they desire to fire the missile to achieve the maximum probability of a kill and still have enough maneuvering room (displacement) to achieve a stern shot if the first shot were not successful.

If I recall correctly, the fire control computer with the AWG 10 did not transition the dot but left it to the aircrew to maneuver for the missile shot. This was due to a preferred solution requested by aircrews.

Phantom aircrews were taught to run an intercept to a Sparrow firing position, then convert the intercept to a stern attack, or stern "conversion." This is required in case the Sparrow fails to achieve a kill, or in the event of multiple bogeys. However, there are times when it is desirable to run a stern conversion only. This is the case in which a rendezvous with a tanker is required, for example, or when it is required to join up with an aircraft to escort it. One example is to join up on soviet aircraft to escort their fly-by over an aircraft carrier, or to visually identify an unknown aircraft at night which would require joining up on it from below without its knowing your position.

Stern conversion intercepts are much easier to run than a Sparrow firing intercept with a stern conversion, but the requirement for the aircrew is the same: to ensure that the aircraft has enough displacement to maneuver behind the bogey.

Displacement can be either horizontal or vertical, or a combination of both. For our example, we'll use horizontal displacement only. Horizontal displacement is the distance from the bogey's extended flight path to the interceptor. The more displacement the interceptor has the more room to maneuver to get astern of the bogey from a forward position. More displacement means an easier turn to maneuver behind the bogey. However, too much displacement may mean that you cannot get to the bogey expeditiously without using more speed which means more fuel, which is not good.

Remember our example of the bogey heading 180-degrees and the interceptor heading 360-degrees. At 60 miles, each degree of target aspect, TA, equals 6,000 feet of displacement. 6,000 feet equals one nautical mile.

At 60 miles:

1 degree of TA =	6,000 feet
2 degrees of TA =	12,000 feet

Target Aspect, TA, is the position of the interceptor from the bogey's nose, or extended flight path. It's how the bogey sees the interceptor. If the interceptor has 5-degrees of right TA, the bogey sees the interceptor 5-degrees right of his nose.

If the interceptor has 30-degrees of left TA, the bogey sees him 30-degrees left of his nose. A surface sailor would say that the interceptor has 330-degrees of target aspect angle. Target aspect angle is the same thing, although it is measured in a relative 360 degree bearing from the ship's bow. At speeds that aircraft fly, and the very dynamic situation involving maneuvering aircraft, aircrews use left or right target aspect rather than target aspect angle.

In the 180 degree TCA example above, displacement remained constant but TA doubled as the range halved. The corollary is that the degrees off collision bearing will double as the range halves. The displacement will continue to decrease on a collision intercept. Steady bearing, decreasing range until collision. The general rule is that for a collision course, the displacement will halve as the range halves.

5 degrees TA at 60 miles = 30,000 feet (1 x 6 x 100 = 6000 x 5 = 30,000)

5 degrees TA at 30 miles = 15,000 feet (1 x 6 x 100 = 6000/2 = 3000 x 5 = 15,000)

Aircrews are initially taught that the best intercept against an equal speed, non-maneuvering target requiring a Sparrow shot with a stern conversion is a 120 TCA intercept:

Collision bearing is 30 degrees (30 x 2 = 60, the MUA; 120 + 60 = 180)

At 60 miles, 30 degrees TA = 180,000 feet or 30 miles
At 30 miles, 30 degrees TA = 90,000 feet or 15 miles
At 15 miles, 30 degrees TA = 45,000 feet or 7.5 miles
At 7 miles, 20 degrees TA = 22, 500 feet or 3.75 miles

Seven (7) miles range is close to heart of the envelope maximum probability of kill firing range for the Sparrow, which still leaves displacement for conversion to a stern attack.

Once the interceptor turns to the firing heading and shoots, it will continue that direction of turn conserving displacement for the final turn to stern quarter attack heading.

The school book solution would be to run a 120-degree TCA intercept until about 10-miles, turn into the target to transition for the firing solution, fire the Sparrow, turn further towards the bogeys stern to conserve displacement, then counter turn to achieve stern quarter attack.

As aircrews get more experience under their belt, the next optimum school solution is the 140 degree TCA intercept:

Collision bearing is 20-degrees (20 x 2 = 40, the MUA is 40; 140 + 40 = 180)

At 60 miles, 20-degrees TA = 120,000 feet or 20 miles
At 30 miles, 20-degrees TA = 60,000 feet or 10 miles
At 15 miles, 20-degrees TA = 30,000 feet or 5 miles
At 7.5 miles, 20-degrees TA = 15,000 feet or 2.5 miles

This "school solution" affords the Sparrow a reasonable probability of a kill with enough displacement, about 2 to 2 ½ miles displacement, to execute a stern conversion attack.

At 7.5 miles the aircrew would fire the Sparrow missile at an approximate heading of 035, turn port hard to place the relative bearing of the bogey at 45 degrees right of the nose, reduce the rate of turn to keep the bogey at that position until about 4 miles or so, then reverse to a starboard turn to essentially parallel the bogey's heading of 180 degrees until another missile shot can be obtained, either the Sparrow or the Sidewinder. Such a stern conversion would place the interceptor into firing position for either missile.

Of course, in the real world the bogey will not fly straight and level unless he must do so to close to a firing position. Once the basics are mastered, the aircrew can maneuver to gain an optimum firing solution compatible with the best tactics for the situation. It all begins with a basic understanding of the intercept spatial geometry.

In the real world of North Vietnam, aircrews had only seconds to find a bandit, maneuver to firing position, attain full systems lock, ensure firing parameters were met, and shoot, all in a highly intensive multiple threat area with friendly aircraft in the vicinity. It all starts with mastery of basic intercept geometry.

By the time I arrived in Vietnam, Navy aircrews had developed tactics by trial and error to maximize the Phantom's strengths and minimize its weaknesses and limitations. Although never told that the tactics we were learning were the result of a formalized study (the study at that time was classified "Secret - No Forn (no foreign dissemination), we benefited from this systematic review of American experience and resultant tactics.

The Red Baron reports were subsequently declassified (in part) and I received the unclassified portion from the Navy via the Freedom of Information Act. Appendix A and B are two examples of successful MiG engagements by F4 aircrews who were obviously well trained. It is this experience which preceded my arrival in South East Asia which provided me and my squadron mates the benefit of hard won experience.

APPENDIX A TO CHAPTER FOUR

Below is a description of an engagement taken from the report which occurred on June 17, 1965, between two F4B Phantoms and four MIG17 North Vietnamese aircraft.

"Six F-4B aircraft (BLUE flight) in three elements were on BARCAP for two strike groups attacking the Thanh Hoa Bridge and the Ninn Binh barracks. The F-4s were in the last orbit after 30 min on station as the last strike group was just completing its attack. The three elements were separated." (This engagement, then involves only one element, 2 F 4 aircraft.)

MISSION ROUTE

Departed YANKEE Station and after refueling from A-3B tankers proceeded to CAP station located about 30 mi NW to Thanh Hoa. The sections were to patrol on a line running from 20-degrees 55-minutes N/105-degrees 45-minutes east."

(Note: this station placed the F4s over North Vietnam in a location which, in 1968, would be a high threat area from SAMS and anti-aircraft artillery.)

"At about 1025H (local time) after being on station at 10,000 to 11,000 feet in a counter-clockwise, NW-SE orientation, race-track pattern in line abreast, 1-1¼ to 1-1½ mi apart, for approximately 30 min, BLUE 1 switched to strike frequency to check when the strike would be completed. One strike group reported that they had finished and another strike group said that they would be finished in 5 min. Lead then went back to the BARCAP frequency, told the flight that they would make one more turn and depart the area at 1035H."

"At approximately 1030H with both aircraft flying at 10,000 to 11,000 ft in a race-track pattern with radar on 50-mi scale, just as they turned to the NW, BLUE 1 picked up a radar contact about 30-35 mi, which was interpreted to be coming from the vicinity of Hanoi or just to the west of it. They went into "ident-attack" formation. The wingman went in a 3-mi trail and the element headed directly for the contact. During the run-in toward the contact, they noted drift on the radar scope and established from that, that the unknowns were on somewhat of a southerly to southwesterly heading. They turned from a heading of about 330-degrees to a heading of about 280-degrees to affect an intercept. (RIO thought intercept course 310-degrees, turning to 280-degrees prior to firing.) The element accelerated to about 550 Kt. They climbed slightly to 14,000 ft and spotted the contacts visually at about 5 mi (four airplanes) 15-degrees to the right. Both RIOs had determined that there were four contacts, and they had determined that they were not locking up on the same airplane. BLUE 1 was locked on the MIG 2 contact and BLUE 2 was locked up on either MIG 3 or MIG 4. The bogeys were cutting across the F-4Bs nose at almost a 90 degree angle, just slightly above at 15,000 ft, just under the overcast; MIG 2 was flying in trail of MIG 1 at about 1500 to 2000 ft. MIG 3 and MIG 4 were in a good section formation in the neighborhood of another 2000 to 3000 ft behind MIG 2. At the same time that BLUE 1 spotted them, they either spotted the F-4s or got a vector in their direction. MIG 1 turned, and came directly towards BLUE 1. BLUE 1 could tell that they were "small silver airplanes," but no positive identification was made at this time. MIG 2, instead of cutting across the corner to join his leader to close the gap, flew the same track over the ground that his leader did. By the time he turned the corner, banked up in a steep bank turning toward his leader, the lead F-4 was close enough to make a positive ID on him. He shouted "MIGs;" BLUE 1 RIO reported "...we are in range. Fire. Fire. Fire." The steering dot was just slightly out of the circle. Lead made a slight turn and fired Station 8, right wing SPARROW at about 2-mi range (RIO reported firing at 3.5 mi). It appeared that the SPARROW went off at about 10 ft behind the MIG 2 tail. At about this same time, MIG 2 rolled up on his wing and there was a mass of flames. Smoke started pouring from the center of the aircraft on aft, and "the whole thing was a sheet of flame." The F-4 wingman saw this also. In the meantime, the second section of MIGs had tended to cut across the corner of this turn and close on MIG 1. The F-4 wingman fired at MIG 3 and his missile hit when MIG 3 was directly above BLUE 1 and MIG 1 (which passed about 500 ft to the left, canopy-to-canopy, of BLUE 1). Neither BLUE 1 nor the pilot of BLUE 2 saw MIG 3 get hit; both were engrossed in the maneuvers of MIG 1. BLUE 2 RIO observed his missile hit a MIG end explode. The MIGs did not appear to fire at any time."

"The F-4s commenced a separation maneuver in AB, flew into the clouds, lost sight of the MIGs, completed the separation maneuver, turned to the left at 30,000 ft and came back out of AB; no radar contacts and no visual sightings were made. They could see the vapor trails of a SPARROW missile. It was obvious that they returned to the same area, but made no sightings or radar contacts. While attempting to reacquire the MIGs, radar contacts were detected to the SE. The F-4s thought it logical for the MIGs to head that way, toward the strike force. BLUE flight headed toward the contacts and identified them as friendly EF-10Bs. BLUE then returned to the firing area. They searched the area and sighted one parachute about 2000 ft off the ground. They were extremely low on fuel and departed the area. BINGO fuel was 5800 lb. and the initial contact had been made at 7000 lb."

APPENDIX B TO CHAPTER FOUR

One more example, taken from an article from Air Combat Command's Combat Edge magazine dated August 1992 about then Captain Steve Ritchie, USAF, encounter over North Vietnam:

"The Day Was 8 July 1972....

"We did not fly the first 6 days in July due to weather. The eighth of July started out as if it would be another one of those days. We were scheduled as the egress flight. The egress flight was the last MiG CAP (Combat Air Patrol) flight inbound with a full load of fuel and armament intended to provide protection for the initial flights coming out low on fuel. There was normally little action for the egress-flight. MiG activity generally occurred early on. We (Paula flight) were grousing about having to get up at 0330, go through all of the briefings, prepare ourselves, the airplanes and weapons, suit up for combat, refuel en route to North Vietnam, jettison the centerline tanks, coordinate with Red Crown and Disco, take a chance of getting shot down and probably not even have the opportunity to engage, and the weather still looked really scroungy.

"Paula flight headed inbound with everyone assuming it would be a routine mission. We'll get in and out, and tomorrow we'll be on the schedule as the ingress flight. About sixty miles from Bullseye (Hanoi), No. 4 in one of the MiG CAP flights was damaged by a hit-and-run MiG attack. He broke formation, headed out, and announced on Guard his position, heading, altitude, and the fact he was losing hydraulics, thus violating a cardinal rule and definitely attracting the attention of the North Vietnamese air controllers. We immediately changed course and headed in that direction.

"About 30 miles southwest of Hanoi, we began getting calls from Disco (the forerunner of AWACS) that there were two Blue Bandits (MiG-21s) in the area. At approximately 5,000 feet on an easterly heading, Paula flight received the 'heads-up' call. 'Heads-up' meant the

MiGs had us in sight and had been cleared to fire. That information was at least 40 to 60 seconds old, and we had no visual on the MiGs. At that point, the Disco controller, some 150 miles away, looking at his radar scope, dispensed with the normal lengthy radio procedure and announced, 'Steve, they're 2 miles north of you.' I made an immediate left turn to north, picked up a 'tally ho' on the lead MiG-21 at 10 o'clock; then rolled further left, blew off the external wing tanks, went full afterburner, and passed the MiG at about a thousand feet, just under the Mach. At this point, we saw only one MiG, but we knew there were two. I rolled level, pushed my nose down, and waited. Sure enough, the second MiG was about 6,000 feet in trail.

'As we passed No. 2, I came hard left into a nose-down slicing turn, about 6.5 Gs, and lost sight of both MiGs. About halfway through the turn, we were surprised to see the No. 2 MiG high in a level right turn. To reduce the high angle-off, I barrel rolled left to his low 5 o'clock position and at about 6,000 feet, maneuvered to put the target in the gun sight, achieved a quick auto-acquisition lock-on (one pulse), and fired two Sparrow missiles. There was a 4-second wait from radar lock-on until trigger squeeze and another 1.5-second delay until the missile launched. Over ninety electronic and pneumatic steps had to take place in sequence before the missile would fire. A 4-G turn was necessary to keep the MiG in the radar field of view as he turned down into us. (The book said 3 to 4 Gs max for a successful launch.) The first missile came off at about 4,000 feet and more than 40 degrees angle-off. We were at minimum range and maximum performance conditions for the Sparrow. The lead missile hit the center of the MiG's fuselage, and the second went through the fireball.

'At this point, Paula No. 4, pulling as hard as he could, managed a radio call, 'Steve, I've got one on me!" The lead MiG had made it all the way around the circle and was almost in Atoll firing position behind Tommy Feezel. We unloaded over the top of the fireball after a piece of debris from the MiG nicked the leading edge of our left wing, selected full afterburner, and cut across the circle to gain a rear quarter position on the remaining MiG, again at about 5 o'clock low. The angle-off was similar to that on the first MiG, but we were closer. The lead MiG-21 was highly polished with bright red stars (every other MiG I saw was a dingy silver). The MiG pilot saw us, forgot about Tommy, and started a hard turn our way. He was a lot better than his wingman and rotated the airplane very quickly. I fired at about 3,000 feet with almost 60 degrees angle-off (the radar breaks lock at 60 degrees) pulling about 5 Gs. Only one missile was fired because we were inside minimum parameters with minimum probability for a hit. The missile appeared out in front, snaking back and forth like a sidewinder, and seemed not to guide. All of a sudden, the missile pulled every available G (approximately 25) and hit the MiG dead center in the fuselage at just about missile motor burnout which accelerated the 435-pound Sparrow to approximately 1,200 mph above launch velocity. "SPLASH TWO."

Reprinted from ACC's Combat Edge, August 1992

CHAPTER FIVE

Operational Readiness Inspection

TRAINING FOR COMBAT IN THE PHANTOM WAS ALWAYS MORE rigorous than the actual combat itself. I don't mean to imply that combat was a piece of cake because it wasn't. Training could not duplicate the real fear, the rush of adrenalin, the stress of actual combat, the confusion resulting in multiple radio calls in a large formation with actual SAMS and anti-aircraft artillery fired in anger. But for the demands placed on the aircrew the training mission was more demanding.

I was fortunate to have been assigned to a fighter squadron that just returned from a combat deployment when I graduated from the Replacement Training Squadron VF 121 in July of 1967. This permitted me the opportunity to participate in a complete training cycle before the next deployment, which was in January of 1968.

The training cycle started out with basic individual flights and progressed all the way through coordinated carrier and air wing exercises which culminated in an Operational Readiness Exercise (ORE) followed by, just prior to deployment, an Operational Readiness Inspection (ORI). Both the ORE and the ORI exercised every part of the Carrier Battle Group's ability to conduct combat operations.

It was in late November or early December of 1967 when VF 96, Carrier Air Wing 9 (CVG), and USS Enterprise conducted the ORI prior to deployment to WestPac scheduled for January of 1968.

The carrier battle group was operating off the coast of Southern California. The Air Wing was scheduled for a large Alpha Strike on a practice target range in the California desert south of NAS Fallon, Nevada. We were briefed that this exercise would be remarkably similar to those Alpha Strikes we would be flying over North Vietnam. This was to be as close to the actual thing as it was possible to simulate.

Enterprise launched the strike late in the morning. The Phantoms tanked immediately after launch, then joined-up with the strike group of some twenty-five aircraft prior to navigating feet-dry (over land), fly through an electronic warfare range to the target, then egress over a slightly different route and recover back aboard Enterprise with a VFR recovery.

Bob and I were assigned as TARCAP. Our mission is to provide fighter escort to the Alpha Strike to the target, accelerate ahead of the strike and hit our targets with cluster bombs which would kill as many enemy personnel as possible, manning the SAM batteries and anti-aircraft artillery, permitting the attack aircraft to better concentrate on striking their assigned targets. After releasing our bombs, we would climb overhead the target area and provide fighter protection. We would then escort the strike group out to feet wet. We were assigned as the wing of a lead Phantom from our squadron. Each TARCAP consisted of elements of two F4 aircraft. There were additional Phantoms assigned to the air-to-ground strike role and to MIGCAP, a strict air-to-air mission.

The launch went as planned without any problems. We joined up with lead, proceeded to the tanker, an A3 Douglas Sky Warrior, topped off, and took our positions in the strike group. The rendezvous of the entire group was accomplished quickly, and the flight started north to ingress north of Los Angeles.

It wasn't long before the group was "bounced" (attacked) by Navy F8 Crusader fighters from NAS Miramar. They came in without warning, attacking the strike birds and anyone else they could gain position on. Our flight of two was jumped by two Crusaders who were flown by experienced, superb fighter pilots. We managed to not be "shot down" initially by the Crusaders, but were unable to gain any advantage on them either. However, in maneuvering with a second attacking element, a third element, unseen by our two ship TARCAP, was "shot down." This was a sobering and humbling experience for Bob and me. Had they been real enemies, the Crusaders would have scored many kills on the strike group. When they disengaged we could not chase them because our rules of engagement precluded us from leaving the strike group. These Navy pilots were extremely aggressive and well trained, more so than our possible North Vietnamese Air Force foes would be. The lesson that I learned from my first day of training was strongly reinforced on this mission, most air-to-air kills were by unseen enemy aircraft. Look-out discipline was critical to survival in a hostile environment.

The Strike Group managed to reassemble and crossed over the beach north of Los Angeles. The route took us over the Navy's Electronic Warfare Range which used actual Soviet radar and equipment which we would face in the skies over North Vietnam. The American crews manning the equipment on the range were skilled at what they did and did not have to fear retribution from bombs or missiles. I remember they gave the entire strike group a thorough workout. All the RHAW gear (RadarHomingAndWarning) in the cockpit was activated. We used all our tactics including ejecting chaff and maneuvering to break lock. It was a demanding task to maneuver with a strike group of twenty-five aircraft while maintaining some semblance of formation and flight integrity. I believe that we were advised during the mission debrief that we would have lost many more aircraft to hostile missiles and anti-aircraft fire had this been in the "real world."

By the time we exited the electronic warfare range, we were at the IP (initial point) for our target. The TARCAP (including Bob and me) accelerated ahead of the strike group and released our practice bombs from a 45-degree dive angle. After release, we circled the target until all the attack Alpha-Strike aircraft completed their attack and were exiting. We then rejoined the group in the rear echelon to escort the group out to "feet wet" (over water).

We were now becoming low on fuel and were looking out for "hostile" aircraft to bounce us again. This time, we were expecting USAF aircraft from the Fighter Weapons School at Nellis Air Force Base. Although Bob and I looked forward to mixing it up with the

Air Force our fuel state was always a concern. Had the Air Force birds shown up we would have been at a tactical disadvantage and would have been "shot down" again. However, the Air Force had to cancel on this particular day. We made it out to feet wet and were vectored to our faithful tanker where we greedily took on the allotted two thousand pounds of fuel reserved for each Phantom.

The daylight recovery was uneventful. The debriefing was in our squadron Ready Room over the Closed Circuit Television from IOIC (Integrated Operational Intelligence Center). The CAG started the debriefing by telling us that we had accomplished our mission but that our real world losses would have been extensive. Had the Air Force bounced us as scheduled we would have lost over half the twenty five planes in the group to both hostile aircraft and ground to air fire. However, CAG continued, it was unlikely that we would face the same air-to-air opposition from the North Vietnamese Air Force. That did not mean that we could let our guard down. He then provided a detailed briefing on what he believed we could do to improve flight formation and integrity under such conditions.

After all the briefing had been completed, Bob and I sat down to go over in our minds the mission. We had been "killed" once by the Crusaders while still feet wet. We had been shot down by an "enemy" SAM during our flight through the electronic warfare range. We managed to hit our target. We stayed with the strike group all the way regardless of our air-to-air encounter and we successfully landed back aboard. We were both sobered by the thought of conducting such a mission in the skies over North Vietnam. At that time, we figured we would have a chance to do so in about three months.

We were fortunate to have never encountered the type of air combat maneuvering over North Vietnam that we did in training. In retrospect, the Navy had prepared us quite well for what was to come.

CHAPTER SIX

Korea

⟡

IN JANUARY OF 1968 I WAS A TWENTY SEVEN YEAR OLD LIEUTENANT Junior Grade (LT JG). I was a "nugget," or an inexperienced aircrew man, on my first WestPac deployment into the combat zone in the Gulf of Tonkin off the coast of North Vietnam. Needless to say, not only was this a big adventure, but a hazardous one as well and I was not only eagerly looking forward to it, but apprehensive about it. I joined VF 96 after it returned from its previous year's deployment to North Vietnam. The squadron lost two aircrews during the previous deployment, both to combat action over North Vietnam. Those returning crews who remained with the squadron and with whom I would make the next deployment served as a repository of hard won combat experience which I eagerly shared.

Enroute to South East Asia we were scheduled for a three day port visit to Sasebo, Japan, before leaving for Subic Bay, Philippines, where we were scheduled to take on our Yankee Station assets. During the transit across the vast Pacific Ocean we were busy attending training sessions. I also spent quite a bit of time in the ship's IOIC (Integrated Operations Intelligence Center) studying the charts of North and South Vietnam, the North Vietnamese Order of Battle, and anything else I could obtain or ask from the Air Intelligence Officers working there.

When the ship entered the harbor at Sasebo we were met by protesters in boats. They were protesting the visit of a nuclear powered aircraft carrier to Japan. However, the visit was peaceful. I was surprised how cold Japan was in January. I believe the day-time temperatures were only a few degrees above freezing.

My roommate was LT Billy Boatwright. A pilot, Billy, spent almost two years in the training pipeline so although he also was a nugget he had recently been appointed to Lieutenant. This was significant because we were both senior enough to rate a two man stateroom instead of being assigned to a multiple-berth junior officer bunk room. We became fairly close.

After the port visit, Enterprise began its southward journey to the Philippines. Billy and I went top-side to the flight deck for a breath of fresh air after the evening meal. I looked out over the water at the calm seas and didn't notice anything unusual. I heard Billy mutter something to himself then ask, "Gene, what side of the ship should the sun be setting at if we're heading south?" I didn't notice until he asked but it became immediately obvious to me that the sun was setting on the port side of the ship! This, of course, meant Enterprise was steaming north, away from the Philippines.

"I'm going to IOIC to find out what the deal is," Billy said as he started towards the edge of the flight deck. "Okay," I replied. "I'll stay up here for a few minutes then head to the Ready Room."

By the time I entered the ready room other aircrews were starting to file in. Although not everyone had been on deck to notice the direction Enterprise was steaming, the word was getting out quickly that something was up. The SDO (squadron duty officer), was busy on the phone calling all the bunk rooms and state rooms to order everyone into the Ready Room for a briefing in fifteen minutes. In response to many questions, the SDO simply said he didn't know and asked that we work down the roster with him until everyone was notified. Soon, the entire squadron was in their assigned seats in the Ready Room anticipating what would be said. The Skipper, Commander Paulk, stood up and told us he had just recently been advised by the CAG (Commander, Air Wing, also a Commander in rank. CAG was a hold-over when the title was Commander, Air Group. It was not appropriate to refer to the Air Wing Commander as the CAW, so CAG was kept.) The CAG advised him that a US Navy electronic intelligence ship was under attack by the North Korean Air Force and Enterprise was steaming at maximum speed to be in a position to render assistance. He then instructed the SDO to turn on the CCTV (closed circuit television). In a few minutes CAG came on the screen from IOIC and reiterated what the Skipper said, then turned the briefing over to the senior Air Intelligence Officer (AIO), a Commander.

The AIO informed us that the USS Pueblo was seized and boarded by the North Koreans and was being taken to North Korea, Wonsan Harbor. As soon as Enterprise was in position to launch aircraft, the Air Wing would be given the mission to assist in the recovery of the captive vessel. He then turned the briefing over to a LT CDR who briefed us extensively on the North Korean Order of Battle.

The Air Wing Operations officer, a LT CDR, then briefed us on the overall Air Wing Mission. The A6 Intruder crews would be given designated targets on the beach at Wonsan. The Phantoms would be given the mission of Air-to-Air superiority. It was made clear to Phantom crews that any aircraft sorting out from the beach would be considered hostile and would be engaged and destroyed. There were to be several strikes. Initially, the strikes would be made at night using only the Intruders as strike aircraft. If and when daylight missions were to be flown, the A4 Sky Hawks from the two Light-Attack Squadrons would be used as well. The Phantoms were to have no air-to-ground missions.

The CAG then stood up and told us that because Enterprise was not scheduled to operate in northern climes there were almost no exposure suits available for aircrews. The order was already dispatched for an emergency requisition for exposure suits (dubbed "poopy suits" by aircrews, presumably because by the time you donned one you were "pooped out"). The CAG regretted that this would decrease survivability of aircrews that were in the water. He then asked the Ship's Meteorological Officer to provide us a weather briefing.

The Meteorological Officer was an older Commander who seemed almost apologetic as he gave us the bad news. We could expect clouds (to be "in the clag") until at least thirty-thousand feet, so we would be in IFR (instrument flight rules) conditions continuously after launch. We would also encounter frequent snow and freezing rain. The flight deck would be hazardous. The combined sea water and air temperature would provide us about three minutes of consciousness before we succumbed to hypothermia. He then implored Flight Deck Officers to instruct the flight deck crews to exercise caution to ensure no one was blown over the deck into the water.

The SAR (search and rescue) detachment OIC (officer-in-charge) followed and gave us the good news. If an aircrew went into the water, a SAR attempt would be made, period. The SAR swimmers were fully equipped with their exposure suits and would be placed into the water. I heard a seasoned LT CDR, Dean Nordell, softly say that it's nice to know that our corpses would be retrieved.

After the briefing, the Skipper stood and told us that we would be in position for launch probably within the next twenty-four hours. He admonished us to get as much rest as possible and to prepare our charts for flights off Korea, to learn of the location of South Korean divert bases, and to ensure our sailors were knowledgeable of what was transpiring and to guarantee they were adequately prepared for cold weather operations. For those officers assigned to the maintenance department, additional preparation of our maintenance crews were to be made to ensure that our aircraft were to be in the maximum state of readiness possible.

I didn't sleep much during the next twenty-four hours. I obtained flight charts from the squadron Air Intelligence Officer and went into IOIC to plot and mark the locations of divert bases, the North Korean Air Bases, and as much other information as was available. Billy and I spent quite a bit of time going over in our minds what type of scenarios we might encounter and how we would react to them. Billy and I were not paired up as an aircrew. My pilot was LT JG Bob Clime. Although a LT JG, Bob was also a nugget, having been an NFO (Naval Flight Officer) navigator on a P2V Neptune ASW (anti-submarine) aircraft. I looked up Bob in the Ready Room and we went over possible missions and what we would do.

I finally went to sleep in the early morning hours and was promptly awakened for the Alert Fighter watch, also referred to as "CONDITION CAP"[6]. The Alert Fighter was in five minute alert

---

[6]   CONDITION CAP - There are three Alert Fighter conditions: Condition 30 which required the fighter to be launched within 30 minutes of the command to launch. Aircrews were permitted to remain in their state rooms or the Ready Room; Condition 15, required a fifteen minute launch from command; condition five, which required a five minute launch from the command to launch.

status which required aircrews to start the aircraft up, complete all pre-launch checks, then shut down with the start gear positioned on the catapult for immediate start and launch. This five minute status required that the aircrew be strapped in the aircraft. However, the Air Boss[7] ruled that after successful startup and pre-launch checks, aircrews could remain in Pri-Fly (Primary Flight Deck Control), that section of the Island in which the aircraft aboard were controlled, out of the elements. I appreciated the Air Boss' decision. As Enterprise steamed further north the weather became progressively worse and we daily encountered snow and freezing rain.

During one Alert Fighter watch, about two hours before dawn, the order came over the 1MC to "Launch Condition CAP! Launch Condition CAP!"

Bob and I walked rapidly to the aircraft from Pri-Fly, we couldn't run because of icy conditions. We strapped in and started up quickly. We completed the abbreviated checklist prior to the catapult shot just as Enterprise turned into the wind and was ready to launch aircraft. I could hear in my headset over the radio that the Angel (SAR helo always airborne during launch and recovery operations) was in the air. I didn't have much time to consider the mission because I was extremely busy with the pre-launch checks.

After the shot in the dark, we climbed to 1200 feet and maintained heading for three miles then arced starboard until intercepting our assigned climb out radial from the ship. I had already painted our wingman on radar and I flew a radar rendezvous on him until Bob had a visual and took position. Although it was still dark, I could begin to see the beginning of first light. The weather officer was correct. We were in the clouds.

After join-up, we switched to the tactical Fleet Air Defense frequency (FAD) assigned to us for GCI and checked in.

"Showtime Six-Oh-Four (604 our Lead's call sign, we were Showtime 605) vector three-three-five-degrees for bogey. Bogey is one hundred miles, angels (altitude) three-zero."

---

[7]   Air Boss - The Air Wing's senior officer in the control tower. Everyone on deck, including flight crews until launched, work for him.

"Six-Oh-Four, roger, three-three-zero," LT JG John Wolfiel replied. John was the RIO in the Lead aircraft. Although on his first tour of duty he made the previous deployment. His pilot, Lieutenant Dick Ernest was also a first tour pilot who made the previous deployment.

At this point, Bob was flying on Lead's wing and relied on me to provide airspeed and altitude information. Hopefully, when it became light we would be able to separate into combat spread formation but with the darkness and IMC (instrument meteorological conditions) all he could do was concentrate on flying the wing position.

I selected the 100-mile scale on the radar,. I didn't expect to pick up an airborne target, but I actually saw it at just less than one hundred miles! It obviously was a large target. We were briefed that the Soviets would send down reconnaissance aircraft. This huge of a target made it likely that the bogey was a Bear, the NATO designation for the turboprop long range bomber, reconnaissance platform the Soviets used to reconnoiter the fleet.

"Showtime Six-Oh-Five, contact 335, ninety-five miles," I radioed.

"That's your bogey, Punch," the controller on the ship replied.

"Showtime Six-Oh-Five, Roger," I answered. The aircraft was still too far in range for me to take control of the intercept by advising "Judy."

"Six-Oh-Five, you take the Lead. Visual my left seven o'clock," Dick radioed.

He was giving us the lead since we had the first radar contact.

"Good job, Gene!" Bob said after acknowledging the lead. "I was getting a little fatigued flying instrument wing."

"Passing twenty-thousand (feet), level twenty-five-thousand, set four-hundred (four hundred knots)," I radioed. "Bogey is dead-ahead, eighty-five miles, angels-thirty."

"That's your bogey, Punch," GCI radioed.

"Six-Oh-Five, Judy, out," I answered. This contact was nice and large and my radar was peaked and in beautiful working order so I took control of the intercept.

"Bob," I said over the ICS. "I'm taking control. We're on a one-eighty (180-degree track-crossing-angle). He's at thirty-thousand. I'm going to run a rear conversion and will start at about fifteen-miles to make it nice and easy. Check your lights on dim and steady."

"Roger that. Dim and steady. You're the boss," he replied, obviously happy to not be flying instrument wing. "I guess Lead's system is not peaked like ours. It looks good up front. We're still in the clag, so Dick is flying instrument wing."

"Check missiles, sweet and safe," I challenged.

"Roger, four and four, up and ready. Switches not armed," Bob replied.

I continued to run the intercept in search mode until 40 miles, providing commentary over the radio for Lead as well as Bob, since John had not yet reported contact. At 40-miles I acquired full-system lock-on. Both radar scopes displayed the attack solution. The bogey was indicating about 400 to 450-knots, level at thirty-thousand feet and maintaining course, 155 degrees, which would take him directly over the ship.

"Six-Oh-Five, bogey is dead-ahead, 35-miles, twenty-five-thousand and descending, overtake increasing to nine-hundred-fifty," I radioed to advise Lead that he was descending for his pass over Enterprise.

"Roger," Dick replied. "I'm left nine-o'clock slightly high. Visibility is better."

"Visual," Bob replied.

Although still in the clouds, it was definitely getting light allowing Dick to put a little more separation between aircraft. The bogey continued to descend, trading altitude for air speed, although certainly not increasing by much. He was three-degrees left at 20-miles. I decided to begin the stern conversion intercept at this point to make it easier for Lead who still had to fly close in.

"Bogey three-degrees-left, twenty-miles, descending through twenty-thousand, overtake nine-fifty. Starboard, go down five-thousand, level twenty," I commanded on radio, beginning the stern conversion.

Both aircraft made a standard rate starboard turn until the bogey was 40-degrees-left. I steadied the flight until he began to drift left, then commanded a port standard rate turn. I also directed the flight to descent another five-thousand-feet and level at fifteen-thousand since the bogey was continuing his descent.

I kept the turn up until he was on our nose and kept him there by varying angle of bank until I noticed that we were coming into his rear quarter. I then varied the angle of bank to give us offset to his left, allowing Bob and Jack to attempt to obtain a visual on him as we closed range to about two miles. A target that large would normally have been visible in the daylight conditions we were now in, but we were still in the clouds.

"Bogey is five-degrees-right, two-miles, descending past fifteen-thousand, overtake is one-hundred," I radioed.

At that point, Dick radioed, "Six-Oh-Four, Tally, right-one-o'clock, slightly high. I've got the lead. Bob, take up radar trail until tally, then take the perch."

Dick ordered us to back off, let him fly visually on the bogey. We were to fly astern of him until Bob acquired the bogey visually, then take a position for an attack by placing ourselves to the rear and above the aircraft.

"Climax," Dick radioed, "We're flying visual on a Bear twenty-five-miles from Home-Plate (the carrier). We're descending below ten thousand, course one five-five-degrees, speed four-twenty."

"Roger, Showtime. Advise visual on Home-Plate, out," the controller ordered.

At this point Dick moved up alongside the Bear. Bob now had a visual as did I. John was busy in the back taking pictures for the Air Intelligence Officers. Often, an aircraft would show an antenna or other configuration that was not seen before so it was important to photograph the airplane for intelligence analysis.

Also, it was imperative that no Soviet aircraft ever fly over an unescorted carrier. That could be construed by some as showing a vulnerability of American carriers to Soviet aircraft. I would photograph the Bear escorted by Lead as we flew over Enterprise.

At about five thousand feet we broke through the clouds and could clearly see the Sea of Japan beneath us. We were ten miles from the carrier. Dick was flying a wing position on the Bear, slightly below him. Bob positioned our aircraft to the left and high enough so that when the Bear flew by Enterprise I could snap photographs of the carrier, the Bear, and the escort Phantom all in one frame, documenting that the Bear did not fly over the ship unescorted.

The photo session went as planned. I shot about fifteen photographs of Dick and John escorting the Bear, five of them flying over Enterprise. I had to be quick to obtain that many photographs. We continued to escort the Bear to about ten miles ahead of the ship, then were ordered to detach and recover. There were other Phantoms airborne now and would keep an eye on the Bear.

We made a normal daylight VFR recovery aboard and when we entered the locker room outside the Ready Room Ensign Pete Heinrich, the squadron AIO, was there to debrief us and take the roll of film from me. Pete was enthusiastic since he also was on his first deployment and this was his first actual debriefing.

When we returned to the Ready Room to complete the Yellow Sheets[8] with the SDO, the Skipper was in his seat talking to CAG. They both smiled at us and said, "Good job, guys."

This intercept was to be only the first of many more that were to follow during the next several weeks while deployed off Korea, although it was to be the only one Bob and I would fly. Throughout the next month Enterprise remained in the waters off Korea, poised to launch strikes against Wonsan when the order came. The order never came. For whatever reason, the National Command Authority decided not to take military action against North Korea for the seizure of an American vessel on the high seas. Billy and I had some lengthy conversations over the incident but our primary focus was on flying, standing watches, and preparing for our tour off Vietnam. We both considered this a blessing in disguise because every flight we accumulated under our belts was more experience we could rely on in combat. An aircraft carrier at sea works seven days a week and conducts flight operations twelve hours a day. The twelve non-flying hours are used for underway replenishment (UnRep), receiving supplies and personnel from the supply ships. We would also frequently refuel our accompanying destroyers which were not nuclear powered.

---

[8] Yellow Sheets - OPNAV Form 3760-2, the aircraft discrepancy or "gripe" form which advised Maintenance what corrective action to take, if any.

The non-flying hours were also used for maintenance and routine operations required to maintain the Air Wing and ship combat ready. I continued to spend many hours in the IOIC not only studying the Korean Peninsula and North Korean Order of Battle, but also that of North Vietnam, our ultimate destination and one which we would inevitably be steaming to soon.

Since the weather was so poor in the Sea of Japan and the Yellow Sea our IFR flying proficiency became sharply honed. An aircraft carrier at sea is a complex and sophisticated operation that requires hundreds of people to perform flawlessly on a continuous basis to succeed. The month of flying off Korea before arriving off the coast of Vietnam paid dividends in the ship/Air Wing ability to operate smoothly and effectively.

The day finally arrived when we were told that our operations in Korean waters would be ended and we would be steaming directly for Dixie Station off the coast of Vietnam. Dixie Station is a southern position which newly arriving carriers would sometimes be assigned in order to provide familiarity flights to aircrews. Although missions flown over South Vietnam were in support of American and South Vietnamese combat operations they were considered less demanding for aircrews than flying in the highly intensive state-of-the-art Soviet air defense system in North Vietnam. This option was provided to newly arriving carriers if there were enough carriers operating on Yankee Station off North Vietnam.

Billy and I were relieved in a sense to be finally approaching our first taste of combat. Although we both had private thoughts about this coming experience we both agreed that the primary fear we both faced was that of not doing our duty. We both knew that others would depend on our performance and we both feared failure even greater than death.

I remember the first day we secured from flight operations and were steaming south. I finally put on my wash-khaki uniform. I mostly kept my flight suit on since flying and standing watches consumed most of our waking time. Things were relaxed. I even watched the movie in the Ready Room, earlier than normal, right after evening chow since there were no flight ops that day. I turned in early and fell asleep quickly. I was suddenly awakened out of a deep sleep at about 0245 in the morning by a messenger dispatched by the SDO. I was initially confused thinking I had overslept a watch then realized that I was not scheduled for a watch and that there were no scheduled flight ops that day. When I was finally awake I asked the sailor why he was waking me from such a good sleep, he replied he didn't know exactly what was up but that something was and I was to report to the Ready Room in flight gear as soon as possible but no later than 5 minutes.

I left Billy sound asleep and snoring as I left my state room and made my way to the Ready Room. I was one of the last people to report, I noticed, because there were about ten other aircrews already sitting and waiting for a briefing to begin. I took a seat next to Bob and asked him if he knew what was up. He shook his head indicating he also had no idea. At that time the skipper, Commander Paulk, entered the Ready Room and all hands stood up.

"Please, be seated," he said. He looked around the room at all of us and then began to speak.

"Gentlemen, we have received word that there is an American submarine close to the Chinese coast that is being closely followed and may be taken under attack by Red Chinese boats and aircraft. If that happens, we will be sent to destroy attacking aircraft and boats."

The Skipper paused to let those words sink in.

"If we are dispatched our job will be air superiority. We will have a missiles-free environment, which means that any aircraft you engage you may destroy without authorization or without visual identification. Each bird will carry four Sparrow and four Sidewinder missiles. You may jettison your centerline tanks when emptied. The problem is due to the distance involved any aircrews that must eject and end up in the water will not be the subject of a rescue attempt."

He looked at the XO, Commander Myers, and said that the briefing over the CCTV will start shortly and for everyone to stand by for the briefing. He then took his seat in the front row.

I looked at Bob, then around to the other aircrews. No one was other than calm, waiting for the briefing to begin, as if this type of mission were just another routine flight and was no big deal.

I also felt calm inside. I appreciated knowing from the beginning that this was a high risk mission and that if we ended up in the water we were on our own. I was not sure yet just how close to the Chinese coast we were but I knew that odds of survival would be low. Yet I was fully aware that my profession required the acceptance of risk. If my country asked this of me I was willing and fully capable of carrying out the mission and would not hesitate to do so no matter what the odds. I believe that everyone else in that room felt the way I did.

Years later, however, I would doubt the veracity of the Skipper's words about not being subject to a rescue attempt if we ended up in the water. I certainly could understand not jeopardizing the ship in order to effect a rescue but if there was any way possible, everything in the American history of combat operations I knew about would lead me to believe that an attempt would be made. Just a brief five months later I would be in the Tonkin Gulf when a Navy Lieutenant and his helicopter would rescue a downed Navy F4 crew over North Vietnam, at night, surrounded by enemy forces and under intense hostile fire. He will be awarded the Medal of Honor. Much later in my career I would also experience situations in which circumstances placed an American serviceman in harm's way and in need of rescue. If there existed any possible means to rescue him there would never be a shortage of volunteers willing to assume even the greatest risk to do so. But if the range was so extreme that a rescue helicopter could not reach a downed aircrew, then it was certainly possible.

In any event, I listened intently to the briefing officer as the briefing began. According to him, the Enterprise was steaming at flank speed to be in a position to launch aircraft. The position of the American submarine was indeed at or near the combat range of our aircraft. However, all aircraft would be refueled en route and in return. The submarine was in shallow coastal waters, could not submerge, and was surrounded by Chinese patrol boats. There were MiG aircraft in the air. It was never clear to me whether the submarine actually was under attack or was just having aggressive action taken against it. When the word came to launch we would join up after becoming airborne and rendezvous with the tankers. After refueling, the strike force would proceed to the submarine's position. When given the order our attack aircraft would take the patrol boats under attack. The fighters would always be cleared to fire against any airborne contact whether visually identified or not. There were some aircrews eagerly anticipating this missile free environment. I was concerned, as was Bob, with completing our mission successfully and returning to the ship.

The missile free rules of engagement would enhance the F4's weapon system. We were thoroughly trained to visually identify hostile aircraft over North Vietnam before being permitted to fire because there were so many friendly aircraft in the skies. Bob and I planned to fire our first Sparrow in the heart of the envelope to maximize probability of kill. The greatest unknown was how much fuel we would have to engage an unknown number of enemy aircraft and still have enough to make it back to the tankers (which would accompany us a great distance).

In the ACM (air combat maneuvering) environment, the mantra ingrained in us was "speed is life." But speed requires fuel. Obviously, the challenges were great.

After the briefing we were told to standby in the Ready Room until directed to man aircraft. After about thirty minutes we were told to proceed to the flight deck and man aircraft. After completing a thorough preflight inspection all aircrews were ordered below to stand by in the respective Ready Rooms until further advised. We went through this drill once more before the word came in that the American submarine had successfully departed the area, was submerged, and was out of harm's way. I returned back to my state room about 1100 and tried to get some sleep. The sequence of the morning events kept playing in my mind, however, so I gave up and went to early chow.

I was never able to obtain further information on what happened that day which caused the American submarine to be harassed by the Chinese but I speculated it was on a special operations mission and therefore classified. In any event, Vietnam would occupy my entire attention for the next five months.

CHAPTER SEVEN

Hanoi

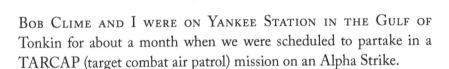

Bob Clime and I were on Yankee Station in the Gulf of Tonkin for about a month when we were scheduled to partake in a TARCAP (target combat air patrol) mission on an Alpha Strike. We flew over the beach on several previous occasions but those missions were in flights of two Phantoms for either air-to-ground or air-to-air missions. The one exception was an earlier Alpha Strike to Hanoi by the Air Wing. On that mission Bob and I were in a four element MIGCAP (MiG combat air patrol) between Haiphong and Kep, the North Vietnamese airfield north of Haiphong located south of the Red Chinese border. On that mission our task was strictly air-to-air and our birds were loaded with four AIM7 Sparrow missiles, four AIM9D Sidewinder missiles plus the external centerline fuel tank. We had a dedicated tanker and were under the GCI control of Red Crown, the Navy's missile cruiser in the Gulf of Tonkin south of Haiphong with the ADIZ[9] mission. That MIGCAP mission had actually been my first over North Vietnam.

The TARCAP mission was acknowledged as a demanding one for Phantom aircrews. I remember, four to six aircrews from our squadron were scheduled for the mission, always flying in elements of two. Our mission was to escort the Alpha Strike formation (called a gaggle) of as many as twenty-five or more aircraft to the target providing air-to-air cover. As the gaggle approached the target the TARCAP F4s accelerate ahead of the strike group and attack the site with cluster bombs. The idea was to kill the SAM and anti-aircraft battery crews

---

[9]   ADIZ - Air Defense Identification Zone

to reduce opposition to the attack crews so they could prosecute their attacks with less "distraction." After we had released our cluster bombs, we were to take station overhead the target to provide air-to-air cover and escort the strike group back out to "feet wet." First in, last out.

I was fortunate to have the benefit of experience of those who previously flew and fought in the skies over North Vietnam. There was a wealth of information that the Navy systematically captured by debriefing returning aircrews and cataloging that experience in "lesson learned" documents which were disseminated to all aircrews. There was also the opportunity to listen to the more experienced guys during bull sessions either at "happy hour" at the Officer's Club on the beach, or in the ready rooms and wardrooms aboard ship.

There had been one other intensive, systematic effort undertaken by the military that I was not to know about until my tour of instructor duty with VF-101, the Replacement Training Squadron on the East Coast at NAS Oceana. That is, I did know about the official study, but the lessons learned in this study were taught to us throughout our training in preparation for deployment to Southeast Asia. We just weren't told what the official source was although there was no doubt in our mind that this experience was frequently hard won through combat experience of those aircrews that preceded us. These were the Secret "Red Baron" reports. The Red Baron reports were the result of a DOD (Department of Defense) effort authorized by the JCS (Joint Chiefs of Staff) by the Office of the Director of Defense Research and Engineering, Weapons Systems Evaluation Group (WSEG).

Recently (2001) I was fortunate enough to learn the Red Baron report had been declassified and was available through the Freedom of Information Act. I was able to obtain a copy of the almost complete report. Some portions remain classified to this date. Currently (April 2015) it is available to anyone off the internet.

To quote from portions of the report:

> Extensive detailed information was gathered from SEA combat aircrew debriefings by specially trained military and civilian teams to supplement the information

contained in the combat reporting systems. The collection data, covering the period April 1965 to August 1967, were organized in outline and narrative formation and also encoded for computer use." The NVN Air Defense System had developed from a rudimentary system in 1964 to a complex, up-to-date, and formidable system in 1967. The weapons employed as part of the air defense system can be classified into three major groups: (1) ground-based guns, (2) surface-to-air missiles, and (3) fighter aircraft."

"The AAA environment encountered in NVN has been extremely dense, particularly in portions of Route Packages V and VI. By the end of July 1967, more than 5600 37mm/57mm guns and 1700 85mm/100mm guns were deployed in North Vietnam. This has had a significant impact on choice of tactics for strike aircraft which, in turn, influenced the altitudes of the protecting fighter force. The antiaircraft artillery capability was further supplemented by surface-to-air missiles."

"The SA-2 was initially used in combat in July 1965. Since that time there has been a steady buildup of prepared sites to a level of 235 sites by the end of July 1967. It should be noted that these are not occupied sites but that approximately 25 SAM battalions move between these sites on a scheduled (but non-predictable) basis. The heaviest concentration of these sites has been in the Hanoi-Haiphong Area, but strategic locations of sites near the DMZ and Route Package V have also been employed by the North Vietnamese to protect these areas."

"The enemy fighter inventory consisting of various versions of the MiG-17 and MiG-21 has remained

relatively constant during the past two years at a level
of approximately 50-60 MiG-17s and 15-20 MiG 21s."

The report is a massive one but serves to refresh my memory of
this particular Alpha Strike. The strike was planned to occur in early
1968 before President Johnson issued his moratorium on bombing
North Vietnam north of the 20th parallel. The CAG himself, a
Commander, was to lead the attack in an A4 Sky Hawk. Other attack
aircraft included the A6 Intruder and the Phantom configured with
GP (general purpose) five hundred pound bombs. As TARCAP birds
we were configured with the "four plus 4" (four AIM7 Sparrows and
four AIM9D Sidewinder missiles) and with six cluster bomb units,
three on each wing station. Of course, we carried the centerline
external fuel tank, which we would quickly jettison if we encountered
MiGs. Other aircraft from the Air Wing included the EA3
Skywarrior in its ECM and ECCM role. Other A3 aircraft would
serve as tankers for those who needed them, including the Phantom
TARCAP birds which would be tanked immediately after the launch
before rendezvousing with the group.

This Alpha Strike was conducted before we received our A6
Standard Arm configured anti-SAM missile birds. At that time we
had only the A4 Sky Hawk configured in its "Shrike" role. The Shrike
was a missile that would lock on to an active SAM site radar and
guide on its electronic emissions to the site effectively destroying it.
The North Vietnamese learned to defeat a launched Shrike missile
by turning off the electronic emissions and turning the antenna 180
degrees away from the threat. The later Standard Arm had a memory
which would continue to track to the target even after the North
Vietnamese ceased electronic emissions.

In addition, the Air Force Big Look aircraft was on station flying
over the Gulf of Tonkin and would be issuing MiG calls on military
guard frequently. Red Crown, the missile cruiser, was also on station
and would also be issuing MiG calls on military guard frequency. A
typical call would be: "Bandits, Bulls Eye, 160 degrees, 30 miles."
"Bulls Eye" was Hanoi, so the bandit call meant that MiGs were
airborne, bearing 160 degrees, thirty miles from Hanoi.

This was the background when Bob and I reported to the squadron ready room for the briefing. The briefing was conducted by Air Intelligence (AI) Officers and the Strike Leaders over closed circuit television (CCTV) to all the participating ready rooms. The AIs, CAG, and the strike leaders were in the IOIC. There were too many participating aircrews to fit into the IOIC, thus the briefing was on CCTV. The briefing began with the CAG saying a few words about how important this mission was and that he believed the Air Wing would conduct a successful mission. The AI officers followed with the Order of Battle which in itself was enough to impress me with the formidable threat we were about to encounter. Then the SAR (Search and Rescue) leader briefed us on what to expect if we were hit and had to eject over North Vietnam, outside of the Hanoi area. If we went down in the Hanoi area it was too risky to send helicopters in to retrieve downed aircrews. However, I was impressed by the intent to try a rescue for any other region outside of Hanoi.

This was the first time that I learned of "friendly" assets to the north west of Hanoi, if we were able to make it over the mountains which included "Thud Ridge."

The strike leader, an attack squadron skipper, briefed the Air Wing on the launch and join-up procedures and the route to the target. The A4 Sky Hawks were so heavily laden that they would have to climb to almost 30,000 feet altitude so they could accelerate by descending, trading altitude for air-speed to the target to ensure they had the maneuverability they required to position themselves over the target and to increase their survivability.

He was succeeded by a LT CDR, an A4 pilot who discussed details of the target with blown up reconnaissance photos as a backdrop. I remember looking at the photos. The target was well within Hanoi, if not right downtown. I remember him pointing out the Soviet and French embassies, a hospital, and the "Hanoi Hilton" where American Prisoners of War were being held.

The item that is most vivid in my memory from that briefing was the LT CDR's statement that if the attack birds could not positively identify their target they were not to release their bombs but keep them until they could reach a designated jettison area to prevent civilian casualties.

After the briefing Bob and I donned our flight gear, checked with the SDO to find the location of our assigned aircraft on the flight deck, climbed the ladder to the flight deck, conducted the pre-flight inspection and strapped into our birds. Once we started our aircraft, we waited our turn to launch. We were scheduled right after the Phantoms assigned to BARCAP (barrier combat air patrol). We would be the first Alpha Strike birds to launch after the tankers because we were slated to top off on fuel prior to the rendezvous with the group.

I remember sitting in the aircraft on the flight deck thinking how many aircraft were participating in this strike. All my previous Alpha Strikes were training missions. Needless to say, my concentration was intense and I was vividly aware of everything happening around me. The adrenalin was pumping.

The catapult shot was normal. We joined up with our flight leader, LT CDR Fran Mezzadri and his RIO, LT JG Garrie Liscum, and ran a radar intercept to our tanker topping off expeditiously. We then took our assigned position to the rear of the strike group; some twenty-two aircraft actually made it. It was impressive seeing all those aircraft flying together as one group.

Once the Alpha Strike was joined the Phantoms never reduced airspeed below 420 knots, "corner velocity", which provided maximum "g" available. Even while still over the Gulf, we had to turn to maintain our position behind the A4 Sky Hawks who were lumbering slowly at three hundred knots to altitude. I already knew more than one friendly aircraft had been shot down by MiGs over water.

Bob and I completed our combat checklist. Bob was concentrating on keeping station on our flight leader, watching out for the position of the strike group, and quickly monitoring his instruments. He depended on me to provide continuous altitude, airspeed, and navigation input to keep him constantly aware of our position and flight. My scan was on the flight instruments, the radar scope which I would switch from air-to-ground mapping mode for navigation and then to air-to-air mode looking for airborne aircraft, including the friendly strike birds, the RHAW (radar homing and warning) gear to analyze the missile and anti-aircraft threat radars, and, of course, outside the cockpit to not only help keep station but to look for hostile aircraft. In all wars, most kills were by an unseen enemy behind an unsuspecting aircrew.

All strike group aircraft were on a common frequency and all monitored military guard frequency. As we progressed "feet dry" (over land) CAG would give instructions concerning position and order. The Nav Lead (navigation lead), an A6 Intruder B/N (bombardier/navigator) provided heading and time to target information. We ingressed south of Haiphong to avoid that city's dense threat. Once we were well over land, Big Look and Red Crown began to give bandit calls on guard frequency. We started to receive anti-aircraft fire and I noted almost constant low frequency chatter in my head set and visual indications on the APR 25 scope with multiple strobe positions pointing to all the radars that were illuminating us. My scan included the "Repeat" light on the ALQ-51.

Aircrews began to call threats by clock code. Several called out SAM tracking information, followed shortly thereafter by the SAM launch calls. I believe it was CAG who commanded "Break Port," which caused the entire strike group to enter into a high "g" left, descending turn, into the SAM missile launch. Neither Bob nor I could see the SAM missiles but I observed the lingering smoke trails after the strike group resumed course back to attack heading. The SAMs missed the group.

We were easily at 450 knots and accelerating. The altitude tactic was successful and the A4 Sky Hawks were descending and keeping speed between 400 to 450 knots.

Radio calls were becoming more frequent now, including several bandit calls from both Big Look and Red Crown. I began to plot the MiG position on my chart but they were still fairly distant to the north of us and heading east. I told Bob that and my opinion that they would be engaging the MIGCAP soon.

We all heard the radio call from an A4 indicating he was hit, descending and was going to eject. We were still distant enough to Hanoi that if he survived he had a reasonable chance of being the focus of a SAR attempt. Then another A4 radioed that he had been hit, was jettisoning his load and aborting the mission. Someone told an aircraft to break off and escort him home.

73

This was followed by several more bandit calls, another SAM launch, and an increasing level of activity on the RHAW gear indicating we were being tracked and fired at by multiple anti-aircraft batteries. There was a call from an A4 that he just launched a Shrike attack against a SAM site followed by a different Shrike bird radioing a second Shrike launch.

I distinctly remember advising Bob that we were approaching our acceleration point at which each TARCAP Phantom would accelerate to 550 knots and pull ahead of the strike group to approach the target. The call came immediately after that from CAG for the Phantom TARCAP to accelerate. Bob was visually locked onto our flight leader and I heard Lead call for burner. The Phantom immediately responded to the CRT (combat rated thrust) and accelerated. Bob and I completed the bombing check list ensuring his switches were selected and the weapons were armed. I remember thinking we were safe from SAM launches now because of the Shrike launches previously but maybe that was just wishful thinking.

Bob's concentration was entirely out of the cockpit keeping position on Lead and looking for the target. I was mostly inside giving him altitude, air speed and heading information. I never ceased to look outside for aircraft approaching our rear quadrant from any altitude.

The chatter from the RHAW gear was continuous, as were the bandit calls from Red Crown. I remember Lead calling a visual on the target and Bob replying visual.

"Showtime 603 is commencing, lead radioed.

CAG acknowledged the call advising the Group to prepare for their attack shortly.

Bob rolled inverted pulling about four gs then rolled upright into a 45-degree dive angle.

At this point I punched out several bundles of chaff in an attempt to transfer any tracking radar from our aircraft to the bigger radar target chaff. I knew we were being tracked by the constant RHAW noise in my headset and the bright intensity of the APR 25 strobes. The ALQ 51 was also constantly in repeat at this time.

I gave him altitude changes in one thousand foot increments and airspeed calls immediately following, since we were descending rapidly. At one thousand feet before release I told him "Standby" then at release altitude, "Mark!" with the release altitude, then "Pull up! Lead is left ten o'clock high going to 9 o'clock."

Bob replied with a visual as he pulled the aircraft's nose above the horizon then jinked hard to the left to spoil any gunner's visual tracking solution. We joined up nicely because Lead turned in towards us to expedite the rendezvous. We both wanted and needed mutual support.

Normally we would have talked to lead reporting visual and trading state (fuel) information but the Strike Group was now rolling in on their targets and the radio traffic increased. It takes expert airmanship to maneuver that many aircraft in a coordinated attack while maintaining flight integrity and safety separation. From my position the attack looked exactly what it was, a superbly coordinated and executed strike.

Bob and I maintained position on lead. We selected the air-to-air missiles and reviewed the check list to ensure we were up and ready. I was in air-to-air mode in the radar and looking in all quadrants for any aircraft. I could see the A4 Sky Hawks and one or two Intruders as they commenced their target run, came off the target, and headed towards feet wet as they joined their elements back together.

I was so busy I did not have time to think much about our position but as I saw the last of the attack aircraft pull off the target and head for home I realized that we were "tail end Charlie" or the last aircraft in the group and were the most vulnerable. We headed for the Gulf of Tonkin. Navigation was no problem. We knew exactly where we were at all times. We kept our air speed at least five hundred knots, constantly changing altitude and heading to spoil optical tracking solutions of the gunners and SAM crews, but always maintaining flight integrity with Lead.

The MiG threat never materialized because the MIGCAP had engaged them shooting down one and causing the others to head for home by diving to the deck and exiting at maximum airspeed. I could hear over military guard that one A4 made it to feet-wet and ejected. He was picked up by Navy SAR helicopter crews. The other A4 ejected over land was never heard from again, not even his emergency beeper, so it was assumed he had been killed or died with the destruction of his aircraft. To my knowledge he was never recovered.

After we went feet-wet we were vectored towards our tanker. I completed the rendezvous by running a radar intercept on him until Lead had a visual (Lead had given us the Lead, (TAC LEAD[10]) since I had been the first to pick up the tanker). It was a good feeling to take on the fuel since we were rapidly approaching "bingo" state and we would not have a ready deck for some time.

We recovered in good order and when we were back safely in the ready room I realized that I was soaked wet from sweating. Although not a smoker, I accepted the offer of a cigarette from my roommate, Billy Boatwright, a chain smoker, back in my state room in an effort to wind down from the tension of the mission.

[10] TACLEAD - the actual leader of the flight due to the best tactical position. MIL LEAD is the designated flight leader.

CHAPTER EIGHT

Sam Launch

I REMEMBER ONLY ONE INCIDENT WHEN I WAS TARGETED AND FIRED at by a North Vietnamese SAM, although I witnessed several shots at other aircraft. The one incident that remains vivid in my mind was during April of 1968. Bob and I were fragged (scheduled) for a Rolling Thunder Mission in Route Package III. The target was a bridge over a river which been was recently rebuilt by the North Vietnamese to keep the flow of men and material moving to South Vietnam. The bridge was about 65 to 70 miles inland, northwest of our IP (initial point or point of entry) on the coast at Brandon Bay. Brandon Bay was a significant feature on the coast of North Vietnam which was prominent on the Phantom's radar, both in ground mapping and air-to-air mode. It was frequently used by me and other Navy aircrews as an IP to target targets in the North.

Our navigation plan was to go feet dry at the southern edge of Brandon Bay, just north of the very prominent karst ridge I frequently used to update the navigation computer. Unlike the A6 Intruder with its SINS (shipboard inertial navigation system) and USAF Phantoms with their INS (inertial navigation system) and LORAN (long range radio navigation) capability, Navy Phantoms had only the analog DR (dead reckoning) computer.[11] Therefore, most Phantom aircrews, and RIOs in particular, were expert dead reckoning navigators. I was fortunate to have been able to hone my skills during the previous months we were flying on Yankee Station. I also spent a considerable amount of my non-flying and watch-standing time in the ship's IOIC (Integrated Operational Intelligence Center) where I could keep track of the constantly moving positions of the manned SAM sites based on the latest intelligence information from aircrews that experienced engagements and from reconnaissance flights. Before our briefing I indicated on my navigation chart the location of the latest information and felt certain our route to the target would keep us out of range of most known active sites. The sites were constantly changing, however, a tactic developed by the North Vietnamese to ensure that they weren't too static to prevent them from being struck.

Briefing, pre-flight (inspection of the aircraft before launch), taxi and launch were normal. The flight would be under VMC (visual meteorological conditions). There were the ever present cumulus cloud formations over the mountains to the west and north.

After the catapult launch we rendezvoused with our flight lead, hit the tanker and topped off (we always had the secondary mission of air to air in the event MiGs were airborne and a threat to friendly aircraft and for that reason we were given the fuel to ensure we would be available during our flight). We were laden with six five hundred pound bombs, three on each wing station; two AIM-7 Sparrow missiles on the aft fuselage stations (which we could fire without having to jettison our centerline fuel tank) and four AIM-9D Sidewinder-missiles, two on each wing. This was our typical ground attack configuration with the air to air missiles.

All systems checked sweet (up and ready) after tanking so we were a go for the mission. Our flight leader was LT JG Charlie Hill and his

---

[11] The AN/ASN-39A is a great circle computer using dead reckoning computations which were only as accurate as the wind vectors and magnetic variation reference furnished the system by the RIO, or the wind vectors furnished by the radar set. Inputs of magnetic heading and true airspeed are automatically supplied by the AN/AJB-3 (attitude reference and bombing computer) and ADCS (Air Data Control Set).

RIO, LT JG Chuck Boehmer, who were on their second deployment with VF-96.

We formed up in combat spread formation, taking station off Lead's wing about one mile to one ½ miles, varying our altitude about 1,000 to 5,000 feet from that of our Lead. Looking out the cockpit I took a second to look towards the North Vietnamese coast. It was a nice day although with the typical haze that was always present. The clouds were scattered, I could see a line of cumulus to the west well beyond our target. We have a clear view of our bridge. We planned to attack individually with a 45 degree dive angle. We would adjust as necessary to any angle if circumstances required, such as a heavily defended target.

I was hunched over the radar scope in ground mapping mode. Brandon Bay and the karst ridge were very clearly distinct on the scope so I updated the navigation computer accordingly. I placed the bridge's coordinates in the target function of the navigation computer so we could steer to it with the number 1 needle. We completed the combat checklist and ready to go feet dry in 3 minutes. Both aircraft switched to a tactical frequency reserved for this mission so we were not hearing much radio traffic, including bandit calls on military guard frequency from either the Air Force Big Look or Red Crown, indicating no MiG activity. At this point Chuck radioed us that he had lost his radar scope and could not get it back.

"Take the lead, Bob," I said. "I've got the Nav lead, no sweat."

"Roger, Showtime Six-Oh-Six, I've got the lead," Bob radioed.

"You have the lead," Charlie responded and took position on our wing.

"Feet dry," I radioed. "Right to two-niner-five (degrees magnetic heading), set four-fifty (450 knots)."

That heading took us to the point at which we planned to attack the target on a heading of 240-degrees which would then let us turn to the south to avoid going further north where there were several active SAM and aircraft artillery sites.

We were at 15,000 feet. Charlie was to our right, about one to one-half miles and at 20,000 feet. I kept him in my scan, although it was the wing man's responsibility to maintain position. I maintained a constant conversation with Bob, advising him of recognizable features, advising him when I was updating the navigation computer, and advising him of distance and time remaining to the target.

We were thirty miles inland steady on 290-degrees at 15,000 feet when I advised Bob that there was a SAM site at left-11-o'clock, 10-miles. IOIC indicated it was not occupied just prior to our briefing so we shouldn't have a problem with it. At this time I heard the characteristic low frequency chatter in my headset which indicated search radar was painting (illuminating) us. I checked the APR 25 scope and saw a broken strobe intermittently pointing to the location of the "abandoned" SAM site. I instinctively punched out two bundles of chaff and radioed to our wingman, "heads up, strobe and chatter, left eleven o'clock."

"Roger," Chuck responded. "We're receiving it too."

"Set five hundred," Bob radioed.

"Roger, five hundred," Carl responded.

At this point, the low warble of the ALR 27 (SAM launch warning indicator) and steady red "SAM" light came on, indicating we were being painted by the SAM acquisition radar.

"Maintain this heading," I told Bob. "We should be able to see the launch and it will give us room to maneuver."

"Agree," he succinctly replied, completely absorbed in looking for the launch.

"Tally, left eleven o'clock low!" Bob radioed, reporting that he saw the launch smoke of the missile or missiles from the site.

"Visual," Charlie responded in an amazingly cool voice.

"Tally one, left eleven o'clock low!" Bob radioed.

"Visual on two!" Charlie responded in a slightly more excited voice.

"Starboard to three one zero, unload, burner, set five-fifty!" Bob commanded.

"Roger," Charlie replied.

At this point, the ALR 27 went into a high frequency, high pitched warble and the red SAM light began to flash indicating that the booster rockets of the SAM missiles dropped off exposing the rear guidance antennas and we were now being tracked by the high PRF (pulse repetition frequency) fire control SAM radar. The APR

25 strobe was also solid yellow pointing to the relative bearing of the launch site. The ALQ 51 light was on and in repeat mode. Our tactic was to push over to about five units angle of attack which would render the aircraft weightless. At that point selecting afterburner would accelerate the aircraft one hundred knots instantaneously. By turning to put the missiles between our 10-o'clock and 9-o'clock position, we were forcing the missiles to pull the maximum amount of lead to complete an intercept with a projected impact point ahead of us on our flight path. At some point decided by the pilot, we would maneuver the aircraft down and into the missiles forcing them to attempt to make a large course correction. The missiles were capable of pulling twenty-five gs, but the radar tracking antenna gimbals were capable of only three gs and, if the tactic were successful, would be exceeded and unable to continue tracking causing the missile to continue to fly ballistically. The optimum maneuvering point depended on the pilot's estimate and the amount of nerve-wracking tension he could take watching those deadly missiles tracking on a steady intercept course.

"Break port!" Bob radioed as he pulled into a descending 6 g turn.

"Roger! Out of burner!" Charlie responded, reminding Bob to deselect CRT (combat rated thrust - afterburner). We needed to conserve our fuel for further maneuvering, if necessary.

"There's three! Visual on the low one between you and us!" Chuck radioed.

"Two are passing us overhead," I radioed. I had a distinct view of two objects appearing to be similar to telephone poles passing overhead.

"They appear to be still tracking you, Charlie!" I advised over the radio.

I immediately brought my scan back into the cockpit. My g-suit was maximally inflated, tightly pressing against my waist, thighs and calves. My head felt as if it weighed sixty pounds (which it did with that much g-force on the aircraft). The aircraft was in heavy buffet. The best way to describe it is to compare it to driving sixty miles-per-hour in an old truck with worn suspension on an Arizona washboard dirt road.

"Passing eight-thousand, five-hundred knots, two-five-zero degrees," I radioed to advise both Bob and Charlie.

"All three passed us and are going stupid," Chuck radioed.

"Reverse to three-one-zero degrees, set five-hundred. Charlie report visual on us," I commanded. The missiles missed and 310-degrees would take us back towards our target.

"Visual. We're your right nine-o'clock high." Charlie responded. He did an extremely good job of maneuvering with us in a high speed, high-g-environment without losing sight of us. What a pilot!

"Tally three explosions right four o'clock high! Must be manual detonations," Chuck radioed.

I resisted the urge to look at the explosions. I had too much work to do.

"Target bears three-one-zero-degrees, thirty-three miles. State (fuel remaining)?" I radioed. I was lucky in picking the heading. The number one needle was right at 310. There was one more karst ridge I should be seeing soon to update.

"Showtime Six-Oh-Five state ten-point-two," Charlie responded.

"Showtime Six-Oh-Six, state-ten-point-five." Bob radioed. Charlie used slightly more fuel keeping up with us, but we were in good shape.

"Going to fifteen thousand." Bob radioed to let Carl know we were climbing back to base altitude.

"Tally on the karst ridge at right one-o'clock-low," I advised Bob over ICS "Good update."

Then over the radio: "Left to three-zero-five-degrees. Target is three-zero-five, twenty-five—miles."

Charlie responded with a double mike click.

The remainder of the flight to the target was uneventful. We reached our attack-bearing in 3 minutes. There were some scattered 23-millimeter rounds visual, but no heavy stuff.

Bob and I completed the checklist, rolled in on a 45-degree-angle dive attack, released and pulled off the target on a heading of 240 degrees. As soon as the nose was level with the horizon, we jinked hard to the left and began a climb to fifteen-thousand feet.

"Showtime Six-Oh-Five off," Charlie radioed. "Visual. We're at your left-seven low, two-miles."

"Steady on one-zero-zero-degrees, set four-fifty. State," I radioed.

"Roger, state seven-point-four," Charlie responded.

"State seven point seven." Bob replied. "Left to-three-three-zero for BDA (bomb damage assessment."

"Roger." Charlie responded.

"Visual. Looks like it's down and in the water," Chuck radioed.

"Roger that!" Bob replied. "Visual. It's destroyed. Good job. Right to one-zero-zero degrees. Charlie take the lead. I'm at your right two-o'clock."

"Visual. I've got the lead," Charlie replied. "Let's keep it at four fifty."

"Recommend zero-niner-zero degrees to avoid the SAM site," I radioed. I was able to get a good update on the navigation computer and could plot an accurate course to steer clear of the site.

"Roger, left to zero-niner-zero." Charlie replied.

RTB (return to base) was uneventful with no further SAM activity. Just anti-aircraft radar signals and light anti-aircraft rounds, mostly at other attacking aircraft. After feet-wet, we checked each other over for battle damage, there was none, then made an uneventful recovery aboard Enterprise. I made sure to brief the duty AIO in IOIC to update the active SAM site chart. It was good to be back aboard the boat.

CHAPTER NINE

Mig Kill

————————

ON MAY 9, 1968, BOB AND I WERE ASSIGNED TO A TWO AIRCRAFT mission as MIGCAP off of the South SAR (search and rescue) destroyer. There were two SAR destroyers assigned off the coast of North Vietnam, the South SAR station was south of Brandon Bay. The North SAR was stationed just off the coast of Haiphong Harbor, on station next to the missile cruiser which had the Red Crown mission.

Red Crown was the code name for the Navy cruiser assigned the ADIZ responsibility between North Vietnam and the American Fleet operating off Yankee Station. The missile cruiser used its radar to cover the skies over North Vietnam. Any aircraft approaching the fleet from the north would have to pass through its radar coverage and if unidentified it would be challenged and, if determined hostile, would be engaged by the ship's anti-aircraft missiles and its dedicated fighter aircraft assigned to BARCAP. US Navy fighters manned the BARCAP twenty four hours a day, seven days a week.

During May of 1968 both US Navy and US Air Force aircraft were limited by President Johnson to bombing targets south of the 20th parallel. I believe this was a gesture aimed at the North Vietnamese for political reasons which have always escaped me, something to do with showing good will. Good will during war was a non sequitur and to the Asian mind a sign of weakness.

Both Navy and Air Force aircraft were assigned military targets in the remaining portion of North Vietnam. This operation was code named "Rolling Thunder." North Vietnam was divided into geographical zones called "Route Packages." Different Navy and Air Force units were assigned specific targets within each route package. The North Vietnamese made good use of this self-imposed American limitation.

The North Vietnamese, under Soviet "advisors," would vector MiG fighters, usually MiG 21 or MiG 17 (NATO designation) towards United States attack aircraft. The airborne and ground/sea controllers advise the attack aircraft of the airborne threat and would "salvo" the attack aircraft (salvo is code-word for attack aircraft to exit the route package). Navy attack aircraft would be vectored south away from the threat from the north over the Gulf of Tonkin. Air Force attack aircraft would be vectored to the west towards Laos or Thailand (or over the Gulf if location dictated. They also had dedicated tankers). The result was the same, the neutralization of attack. Initially, Navy aircraft, when warned of the MiG threat, jettisoned their bombs and other ordnance in an attempt to permit better maneuverability and fuel consumption during high speed evasive maneuvers.

To counter this MiG threat without providing each attack element dedicated fighter escort, the Navy positioned a MIGCAP off the South SAR. When the attack aircraft were "salvoed" the MIGCAP would be vectored towards the southbound MiGs. Once the attack aircraft exited the Route Package the MiGs had accomplished their mission of neutralizing the threat and would return back to the north across the 20th parallel. Even if the MIGCAP could catch them the rules of engagement in effect at that time prohibited crossing the 20th parallel.

The Navy soon determined that the MiGs intended only to drive the attack aircraft away and would return north as soon as that objective was obtained. As soon as Navy fighters were vectored towards to intercept the MiGs and closed to a certain distance, the MiGs turned north. The Navy learned to salvo the attack aircraft without jettisoning their bomb loads and would return the attack aircraft back into the Route Package when the fighters were in pursuit of the north bound MiGs.

To counter this American tactic the Soviets and North Vietnamese developed "pouncer" tactics. When the MIGCAP were vectored in the

MiGs would not turn north but west, placing the pursuing American fighter aircraft into a tail chase. A second element of two to three MiGs would then be vectored towards the American aircraft in pursuit making a slashing high speed attack under GCI (ground control intercept) from the blind side, from a higher altitude, and out of the sun if possible. These tactics were right out of the Soviet air defense tactics handbook.

This was the situation during the afternoon of May 9, 1968, when I left the ready room aboard Enterprise for the flight deck with my pilot, Lieutenant, Bob Carter. (Bob and I were promoted to LT from LT JG at the same time in March of 1968. He was previously an NFO, a navigator on the P2V Neptune. I was previously a surface officer stationed on a small ship. We were more senior than our squadron mates with whom we trained. Our section leader for this event was Air Force CAPT Jack Heffernan and Navy LT JG Frank Schumacher. Jack was an exchange officer serving a tour with the Navy. Selected pilots and aircrew were exchanged by the two services to ensure that some continuity of tactics and sense of community were kept between them. Frank Schumacher was a second tour RIO who was with VF-96 on the cruise the year before.

VF-96 flew the McDonnell F-4B Phantom II equipped with the APQ-72 airborne radar, a pulse radar which preceded the Pulse Doppler radar of the F-4J. I considered the South SAR MIGCAP mission a piece of cake. We were not scheduled to fly over North Vietnam with its state of the art Soviet anti-aircraft defense missiles, anti-aircraft artillery, and hostile MiGs. Secondly, we carried a full complement of air-to-air missiles, four Sparrows (AIM7) and four Sidewinders (AIM9D). We were unencumbered by air to ground ordnance (bombs and rockets) so our maneuverability was better. And last, but certainly not least, if we were to be vectored against MiGs we would have a dedicated airborne refueling tanker. The Phantom was a fuel burner especially in Combat Rated Thrust (CRT), or "afterburner" consuming fuel at about 12,000 pounds per minute! Phantom crews were always sweating fuel. I was on several of these. Normally we would orbit over the South SAR destroyer (a DD) for about an hour and a half then be sent home for a daytime carrier recovery.

However, just like every other mission, we always prepared for the worst case scenario. Bob and I carefully conducted the pre-flight inspection on our assigned war bird (Bureau number 151498) ensuring the missiles were installed and rigged and everything else on the aircraft was in order. Start-up and taxi were normal and all systems checked sweet. The catapult shot was routine and we were cleared to rendezvous with our flight leader, proceed to the tanker and top off on fuel. When we checked in with the South SAR DD we were in good shape: all systems on both birds up and ready and a full bag of fuel. If during our orbit we were to drop below a certain fuel level a tanker would be vectored in to top us off.

We were anchored port, Navy talk for a lazy left turn orbit in "max-conserve" (maximum fuel conservation power settings on the throttles) for about fifteen minutes before anything unusual happened. We orbited at five thousand feet to give us a better radar look up capability. During this part of the day there were numerous cumulus cloud buildups to the west over North Vietnam which cluttered our radar scopes making detection of aircraft difficult. Since MiGs would be attacking from higher altitudes by looking up we could reduce "ground clutter" (radar return from the sea and ground), eliminating some of the undesirable return. Bob and I were talking casually with our oxygen masks off, one strap loosened so the mask hung loosely on our faces, but still allowed us to talk by pressing the inter-com "press to talk" switch. This setting is referred to as "cold mike." As we turned in our orbit facing the west and North Vietnam I would search the scope for aircraft then update the airborne navigation computer by using prominent land points on the coast. We had a dedicated radio frequency so were not able to listen to the other aircraft operating over the North unless they came up on military guard frequency, an emergency radio frequency which all aircraft and ships monitored.

It was about this time that the friendly voice on the DD asked us to switch to encrypted radio frequency on the KY-28.[12] We did so activating the encryption mode and checked in when the system indicated synchronized and activation completed. The controller told us that MiGs were vectored southbound and if the salvo order came we

---

[12]   KY 28 - the electronic voice radio scrambler; encryption codes were changed daily

would be vectored in "hot." This meant that when all friendly aircraft were out of harm's way and were accounted for, we would be cleared to fire when engaged without the necessity of obtaining a visual identification of the enemy aircraft. Normally, there were so many friendly aircraft over the North that fighter aircraft were required to visually confirm that hostile aircraft were indeed the enemy to preclude shooting down friendly aircraft. This rule of engagement neutralized the forward firing capability of the Phantom's AIM7. It also put the Phantom crews at a disadvantage against the tighter turning MiG. The key to overcoming this disadvantage was to have maximum speed during the visual identification maneuver. Normally the MiGs would not engage (there were exceptions) but after one slashing attack would normally turn home at maximum speed and dive to the deck to get lost in the ground clutter.

The DD air controller also advised us that we wouldn't have time to return to encryption mode and that the vector would be in uncovered voice. We returned to normal radio and awaited further developments. Jack asked us our fuel state and we responded. The external centerline tank was empty and we had a full internal fuel load. Jack advised that if we were to get a vector we would jettison the centerline tank. To avoid damaging the tank and the aircraft, the forward AIM7 Sparrow missiles were disabled from the firing circuits with the centerline aboard. Without the tank they were in the firing sequence. In addition, with the centerline tank aboard we were limited to 660 knots air speed.

The next few minutes were quiet. We were now flying a figure eight pattern oriented parallel to the North Vietnam coastline to afford us the maximum look with our radars. I remember quite a bit of clutter on the radar scope and thought that it would be difficult to pick up an aircraft at any distance within that heavy clutter.

Then the words came over the radio in a calm, professional manner.

"Showtime Six-Oh-Two (Jack's call sign), vector two-six-zero (degrees, magnetic compass heading) for bogey. Your bogey is two-six-zero degrees, forty-five miles."

Jack immediately made a high-g turn to the heading and radioed, "Showtime Six-Oh-Three (our call sign), punch off the centerline, NOW!"

I immediately felt the aircraft lurch when freed from the aerodynamic drag of the empty centerline tank. Immediately after the vector Bob and I locked our oxygen masks on, selected "hot mike" (open intercom so we could communicate between cockpits without pressing the "press to talk" switch). The intercom was set at a threshold which would activate it when either of us spoke eliminating cockpit noise when in the listening mode.

I hunched over the radar scope and selected fifty-mile scale with a slight look up avoiding as much ground clutter as possible. I told Bob to stand by for the combat checklist which we covered in a challenge and response manner:

"Fuel?"

"Wings selected, state eleven point five." (Eleven thousand five hundred pounds of fuel)

"Missiles?"

"Armed and ready. Four and four." (Four AIM7 and four AIM9D)

"APR - twenty five, on." (I controlled the electronic warfare electronic counter measures (ECM) equipment.)

"ALR - Twenty Seven, on."

"ALQ - Fifty One, on and in repeat."

"Chaff doors, open and ready."

At this time we were in "combat-spread" formation. We were positioned about a mile to the north, or right of Jack and Frank, and one to five-thousand feet above. It was imperative that we maintained our position for mutual support. Our duties therefore consisted of ensuring that we always maintained visual contact with our flight leader. Bob spent most of his scan outside the cockpit, keeping position on the leader, looking ahead for aircraft, inside the cockpit to quickly monitor his instruments and then back outside.

My scan was on the radar scope, then to the flight instruments to check air speed and altitude, then outside to check position on lead and then back again to the scope.

"Passing two-five-zero for two-six- zero," I told Bob. "Five-hundred knots, passing six-thousand (feet of altitude)."

"Showtime, your bogey is two-six-five-degrees, thirty-seven miles," the air controller in the DD said in a calm voice. "All friendly aircraft are salvoed."

"Come right to two-six-five-degrees climb to eight-thousand. Set five-fifty (knots)," Jack said over the radio.

"See anything yet?" Bob asked.

"No," I replied. "Advise when feet dry."

"Your bogey is two-six-four-degrees, thirty three miles," the air controller radioed.

"Feet dry," Bob advised.

I quickly glanced outside the cockpit to see the south side of Brandon Bay. I recognized the karst ridge to the south and knew that the city of Vinh was just to the southwest of that. That gave me an opportunity for a quick navigation computer update. Then I immediately returned to the radar scope. The clutter was extremely heavy, the bright yellow return of the cumulus clouds filling the entire fifty mile scope display. I saw three very prominent blips to the right about thirty-five-degrees from our nose. Everyone was thoroughly briefed on the North Vietnamese tactics so it was unnecessary to voice the fact that we were being tracked by pouncer MiGs as we pursued the original MiGs to the west.

"Contact, thirty-degrees-right, twenty-nine-miles!" I called over the radio.

"Come right to two-niner-zero! Go gate (select afterburner), set six-fifty (knots)!" I commanded. All commands were now over the radio. I wanted the most speed we could get to engage.

"You have the lead," Jack radioed.

"I've got the lead," Bob replied.

"Showtime Six-Oh-Two," Coolidge (South SAR DD) radioed, "you're cleared to fire!"

We were now the tactical flight leader and Jack and Phil were flying off our wing in combat spread formation.

"What's our altitude?" I asked Bob over the intercom.

I was concentrating on the blips, noticing that they were descending which required that I constantly make small corrections of the radar antenna with the elevation wheel on the radar hand control. I could not afford to lose them off the screen by looking away at the altimeter.

Before Bob could reply I attained full-system lock-on (automatic antenna tracking and display of the fire control solution system on both radar scopes).

"Right to three-zero-zero, contact dead-ahead, twenty-two miles, overtake twelve-hundred-knots." (Overtake is relative closing velocity which would have been about 1300 to 1400 knots if the MiGs and us were in a head on closing situation. The 1200 knots relative closure indicated that they were turning away, in their expected evasive maneuver to avoid engaging us.)

This radio transmission advised Jack and Phil that I had the full system lock which is necessary to guide the AIM7 Sparrow to its target.

"Set six-hundred", Bob radioed. Then, in the cockpit to me, "Gene we've got six hundred knots which is plenty." (He didn't have to tell me that we were sucking fuel at an alarming rate.)

"Passing fifteen-thousand, go down-five-thousand. Contact is four-degrees-right, eighteen-miles, overtake decreasing, passing nine hundred knots. They're descending and in a turn to the right!" I radioed.

It was obvious that by now the MiGs were taking evasive action. It was also obvious from the attack display on the radar scope that we were rapidly approaching maximum shooting range of about twelve miles.

"Contact dead-ahead, twelve-miles, overtake decreasing past six-hundred knots. Shoot! Shoot!" I radioed, although my advice to shoot was only to Bob and not to Jack. At this point there was not enough time to make two separate transmissions.

"Look at that circle!" Bob exclaimed over the intercom. The electronic generated attack-display included an "in-range" circle which was at maximum diameter indicating that we were in the heart of the firing envelope which gave us the best probability of kill. It was a small circle beyond maximum firing range then gradually widened to maximum diameter in the heart of the firing envelope, then would rapidly decrease as minimum firing range approached. It was wide open indicating optimum shooting range. Very shortly it would start to contract indicating approaching minimum firing range with much less probability of a kill against a maneuvering aircraft.

"Fox One!" Bob radioed the radio call for firing the AIM7 missile.

"Fox One!" I heard Jack exclaim over the radio, indicating that he had also fired an AIM7 missile.

"The first Sparrow just went stupid!" I heard Bob say, but I'm not sure if it was over the intercom or over the radio.

"Shoot!" I implored.

"Fox One!" Bob radioed again.

"Look at that sucker track!" Bob exclaimed over the intercom.

"We got him!" I heard Jack radio. "I see a ball of fire!"

"What's it doing?" I asked Bob, referring to the second missile. At this time I broke my visual lock on the radar scope. I noticed that the visual ECM warning indicators in the cockpit were lit-up like a Christmas tree and the audio-warnings in my headset were loud and continuous. I tuned them out in my concentration on the radar scope. We were being tracked by anti-aircraft radar as well as SAM (surface to air missile) radar. I looked out the cockpit to get a visual on Jack but my scan was diverted by the sight of a wide array of exploding anti-aircraft rounds too close for comfort, eighty-five millimeter rounds.

"We're being tracked by the entire country!" I advised Bob. "Did you get a visual on the MiG (meaning did you visually confirm the kill)?"

"I followed the missile well after it left but lost sight of it when I attempted to find Jack," Bob replied.

"Break port! Lead is at our left seven o'clock low, in a descending turn," I advised Bob.

I felt six-g's as Bob yanked the Phantom into a descending left turn, taking a position on Jack's left 7 o'clock position, about five thousand feet above him. As soon as we began the turn I pumped out several bundles of chaff hoping to break lock of the enemy anti-aircraft radar by shifting it from our bird to the chaff. It worked.

I didn't realize the implications until later, but Jack had actually been obligated to stay on our wing since we had taken the tactical lead. At least until he took the lead back or we gave it to him. I don't remember addressing that point. There may have been a transmission made that I didn't hear. In any event we joined up on Jack and Phil but couldn't advise them that we were aboard and that Jack had the lead because he was on the radio.

"Coolidge, Showtime requests a vector to feet wet. Request you start a tanker," Jack radioed the South SAR DD.

At this time we were already heading east towards the Tonkin Gulf, obviously by its different radar return on the scope. The Tacan broke lock so I selected Nav Comp (navigation computer). The number one needle was pointed towards Enterprise's position.

"Roger, Showtime, vector zero-eight-zero-degrees for feet-wet. Raygun Five-One-Five (the airborne A6 tanker) is anchored port, zero-eight-zero-degrees, fifty miles. You're cleared to top off."

"Roger," Frank responded. "Zero eight-zero-degrees. Bob, what's your position?"

"Your left eight-o'clock high, two-miles. We'll be aboard as soon as we steady on zero-eight-zero," Bob replied.

"Showtime, you've got MiGs at your six o'clock, thirty miles," the air controller advised.

"I've got the lead," Jack radioed. "Bob, start an S-turn to clear our six."

"Roger, you've got the lead," Bob replied and began a rapid turn to starboard.

We did the "S" turn maneuver to clear each other's six o'clock position. The original flight of MiGs we were vectored to reversed course towards us when we turned to engage the pouncer MiG flight. However, they were thirty-miles away and we were at five hundred knots airspeed. There was no way they could catch us before we went feet wet and the US Navy owned the Gulf of Tonkin. They would soon break off and head for home. But we weren't taking any chances.

At this time we were getting low on fuel and approaching "bug out" state, or that fuel level which required high speed disengagement and return to feet wet. As we crossed the coast we throttled back to max-conserve power settings, joined up, and after checking each other over for battle damage, rendezvoused with the tanker to take on full internal fuel. We stayed at fifteen thousand feet. After tanking we headed back to the carrier for a VFR recovery. (Daylight, visual flight conditions when landing on the carrier which was conducted in "zip lip," or minimum radio traffic.)

As we headed towards Enterprise, we were instructed by the South SAR DD to switch to encrypted frequency. When we checked in we were advised that the pouncer MiG formation originally consisted of 3 MiG 21 aircraft. After we fired our missiles only one remained and was tracked back to home base by the "spooks" that monitor such things. Because Jack had actually seen his MiG burst into flames he and Frank received a "probable" kill (you must have an independent witness to the destruction to get a confirmed kill.) Because Bob broke his visual concentration of the missile to locate Jack and did not actually see the missile impact the MiG, we were credited with only a "possible" kill. I couldn't see the MiG at that range from the rear cockpit. That was also the time I became acutely aware of our being tracked by numerous anti-aircraft and SAM radars.[13] The Air Controller on the South Sar DD seemed certain of his information that three MiGs were tracked down in the attack but only one was tracked after the engagement.[14]

Because we had just returned from a successful MiG engagement, and because we had plenty of fuel, Enterprise permitted us to be the last two aircraft to recover aboard. We were also permitted to approach overhead the ship individually at 450 knots (we were actually at 450 plus) and execute a "victory" roll overhead so everyone on deck knew we were coming home with a kill. Not only that, each pilot was automatically awarded an "OK 3" carrier landing grade, regardless of the actual recovery. (Each carrier landing is graded. An "OK 3" refers to a good landing which results in trapping the number-3, or target, landing cable. It is the best grade possible.)

After recovery, we were taxied and parked forward of the "island" (that part of the carrier's superstructure which is above the main deck, or landing deck.) When we exited the aircraft we were told to pose for several photographs taken by the ship's Photographers' Mate. The picture attached to this memoir is one of those.

---

[13]   At least one fireball and smoke plume was observed and radar evidence after the engagement showed that only two of the three targets remained. www. scalerjes.com

[14]   Later (2024) I read in an unclassified summary that the pouncers we encountered might have been PLAF (People's Liberation Army) aircraft. The US did may not have desired to become involved with a conflict with the Chinese and did not pursue any further publicity.

I'm kneeling in the first row, six from the left. Bob, my pilot, is kneeling next to me

Official US Navy photograph of Bob Clime and me after recovering aboard Enterprise after our MiG kill. My father inadvertently wrote the wrong year 'sixty-seven on the bottom of this copy which I sent him in a letter.

CHAPTER TEN

Search And Rescue (SAR)

DURING THE VIETNAM WAR THE UNITED STATES DEVELOPED AN excellent search and rescue capability. I frequent attended briefings involving American SAR efforts, especially over North Vietnam. I was impressed with the organization the Air Force had in place. The men involved were far and above the most valuable element of all the dedicated assets the services gave to the SAR effort.

I knew if I were shot down over North Vietnam an attempt would be made to rescue me unless it was impossible to do so, or if the risk of losing rescues forces was exceedingly high.

During June 1968 Enterprise was on her last line period of the deployment. We were scheduled to leave the line on Yankee Station on the last day of June, return to Subic Bay to unload and transfer our Yankee Station assets, then return home. That last month was a busy one for VF 96, each aircrew flying at least once every day.

I remember one day vividly, June 19, my 27th birthday. Looking at my flight logbook I see that I flew a mission coded "1W2", daylight combat air patrol, or CAP. My roommate, Billy Boatwright, was scheduled for "4W2", or night time, visual flight rules, CAP. I don't remember the details of my mission, but the details of Rich's mission remain memorable to me because he described it in great detail.

Rich was on BARCAP that night when he and his RIO, LT JG Ken Roberts listened to a SAR effort by a US Navy helicopter crew to rescue a downed Navy Phantom crew from another carrier. Because much of the rescue effort was made on military guard frequency, Rich and his RIO listened to almost the entire mission. The pilot and aircraft commander of that helicopter aircrew was Lt Clyde Everett Lassen who received the Medal of Honor.

The MEDAL OF HONOR to
Lieutenant Clyde E. Lassen, United States Navy
For service as set forth in the following

CITATION

For conspicuous gallantry and intrepidity at the risk of his life above and beyond the call of duty on 19 June 1968 as pilot and aircraft commander of a search and rescue helicopter, attached to Helicopter Support Squadron Seven, Detachment One Hundred Four, embarked in USS Preble (DLG 15), during operations against enemy forces in North Vietnam.

Launched shortly after midnight to attempt the rescue of two downed aviators, Lieutenant (then Lieutenant, Junior Grade) Lassen skillfully piloted his aircraft over unknown and hostile terrain to a steep, tree-covered hill on which the survivors had been located.

Although enemy fire was being directed at the helicopter, he initially landed in a clear area near the base of the hill, but, due to the dense undergrowth, the survivors could not reach the helicopter. With the aid of flare illumination, Lieutenant Lassen successfully accomplished a hover between two trees at the survivor's position. Illumination was abruptly lost as the last of the flares were expended, and the helicopter collided with a tree, commencing a sharp descent.

Expertly righting his aircraft and maneuvering clear, Lieutenant Lassen remained in the area, determined to make another rescue attempt, and encouraged the downed aviators while awaiting resumption of flare illumination. After another unsuccessful, illuminated, rescue attempt, and with his fuel dangerously low and his aircraft significantly damaged, he launched again and commenced another approach in the face of the continuing enemy opposition.

When flare illumination was again lost, Lieutenant Lassen, fully aware of the dangers in clearly revealing his position to the enemy, turned on his landing lights and completed the landing. On this attempt, the survivors were able to make their way to the helicopter. Enroute to the coast, Lieutenant Lassen encountered and successfully evaded additional hostile antiaircraft fire and, with fuel for only five minutes of flight remaining, landed safely aboard USS Jouett (DLG 29).

His courageous and daring actions, determination, and extraordinary airmanship in the face of great risk sustain and enhance the finest traditions of the United States Naval Service.

Lieutenant (Junior Grade) Clyde Everett Lassen was the Officer in Charge of Detachment 104 of Helicopter Support Squadron SEVEN (HC-7), the "Sea Devils," aboard *USS Preble* (DLG-15). The assignment was Combat Search and Rescue.

Billy told me in our stateroom the next day he could hear rounds of enemy fire striking the helicopter when the aircrew keyed their radio to speak on military guard. He also told me that the pilot and RIO were separated. The RIO was on a heavily wooded hill, the pilot was further down the hill. There was a force of North Vietnamese military between the pilot and RIO. Both the pilot and RIO were talking to the helicopter crew with their survival radios on military guard so Billy and his RIO could hear the three way conversation.

After several attempts, each made with radio transmissions, many of which relayed the rounds of enemy fire striking the helicopter, the crew successfully picked up the pilot. At this point, the RIO radioed that there were too many North Vietnamese between him and the helicopter and he could not reach their position. He ordered the helicopter to leave him and return to the ship. The pilot radioed that he was not leaving but was coming to the RIO's position. LT (jg) Lassen then lifted off, flew over the North Vietnamese taking additional rounds of fire, and landed on the heavily wooded hill permitting the RIO to run to his position and be recovered aboard. I'm not sure how many times Lassen turned on his landing lights, but from Billie's description it could have been twice.

The helicopter managed to successfully egress over land to the Gulf of Tonkin where they recovered on the Jouett, the North SAR DD (in this case, DLG). They truly did have only five minutes of fuel remaining. No less heroic, in my mind, were the entire aircrew of that helicopter.

I was deeply affected then by this valiant display of heroism, and I am still deeply touched by it. I was involved in SAR attempts as the closest available aircraft. Normally our flight lead would take low station to mark the aircrew's position and attempt to intimidate responding North Vietnamese ground forces, while Bob and I would take high station to relay radio traffic and serve as a an air-to-air Tacan navigation aid for responding SAR forces. I listened to more than one rescue attempt, some successful, some not. In each case the responding SAR aircrews would take whatever action necessary to attempt a rescue, even if it meant placing themselves in great jeopardy.

After I retired and returned to Tucson, I read an article in the Arizona Daily Star in the spring of 1993. The article was about a retired Navy pilot named Donald West who was Lt. Lassen's co-pilot on that rescue attempt. The reporter of the Star was interviewing him at his job at the Aerospace Maintenance and Regeneration Center at Davis-Monthan Air Force Base here in Tucson, Arizona. In that article Donald West was quoted as saying he had come across the first helicopter he had flown for the Navy 26 years ago. I quote from the article:

> "West has forty-six ribbons and medals. He has logged 3,500 hours of flight time without an accident. In June, he will be in Florida for the 25th anniversary celebration of a 1968 rescue he took part in during the

Vietnam War. A helicopter similar to the Seasprite that West found at Davis-Monthan was used in the rescue.

"It was the most heroic rescue the Navy has ever done," Donald said. "It was midnight in North Vietnam when we got a call that one of our F-4 aircraft went down". We suited up and went twenty-one miles inside North Vietnam. We attempted to extract two pilots from on top of a hill by using a force penetrator (a hoist). As we attempted to lower the penetrator, the flares went out, leaving us in total darkness. We decided to (ease up) and we hit a tree and our cargo door came off. We finally got airborne away from the hill and communicated to the pilots to get off the hill. We found a spot to land. All this time we were being fired at with semiautomatic (weapons) and machine guns. With the intense fire going on and no pilots in sight, we elected to lift up and circle overhead. At this point, I noticed a fireball coming towards our port (left) side and it just missed us. It was a surface-to-air missile. We elected to make a third attempt to land and the Charlies (the North Vietnamese) were real mad. We put our lights on and the pilots came from under brush running towards our (helicopter) and one of them tripped and broke his ankle. They made it and we turned our lights off and we flew out of there as fast as we could. We landed back on the ship with five minutes of fuel left."

Men like Donald West and Clyde Lassen are heroes. I have been privileged to meet and serve with many others who would quickly volunteer to encounter danger for the purpose of rescuing fellow American servicemen. I served with many of these men in my tour with JSOC. One mission in particular in which I participated in the planning remains in my mind. But that is another story.

CHAPTER ELEVEN

HMAS Hobart[15]

ONE OF THE MORE UNEXPECTED INCIDENTS I WAS INVOLVED IN occurred on the night of June 16, 1968. Bob and I were scheduled for a late night armed reconnaissance mission over Route Package III. This particular mission was not a highly effective one. The Phantom's air intercept radar was not conducive to low-level radar navigation and the enemy was difficult to locate at night. I believe that Enterprise was operating on the midnight-to-noon schedule. In my experience there were always at least two carriers operating on Yankee Station. One operated from midnight-to-noon, the other operated from noon-to-midnight.

As we approached the catapult we were advised that after launch and departure we were to switch frequencies to Strike (control) for a new mission. The cat shot was normal. We cleaned up and climbed to 1200-feet, proceeded straight ahead to 5-miles, then began a right turn, arcing at 5-miles until we intercepted our outbound radial and began our departure on that radial while climbing to 15,000-feet. When I switched to Strike control frequency and checked in Strike requested status of our radar and missiles. After I replied that we were operational in all respects we were told to vector south on a heading of 210-degrees to jettison our air-to-ground ordnance, which I remember as six 500-pound general purpose bombs and two 5-inch Zuni rocket pods. When directed to do so by Enterprise we jettisoned our ordnance and were vectored on a heading of 180-degrees. We were directed to proceed to the vicinity of Tiger Island and contact a GCI

---

[15] Her Majesty's Australian Ship; an Australian guided missile destroyer

(ground control intercept) unit near DaNang on an assigned frequency and conduct air-to-air operations as directed.

I was familiar with Tiger Island. Its Vietnamese name is "Hon Co" and it is off Cape Lay (Mui Lay), just northeast of the 17th parallel, which is the demarcation between North and South Vietnam, the DMZ (demilitarized zone). It is very prominent on the Phantom's radar and I previously used it to update the navigation computer before going feet dry for missions over South Vietnam or Laos.

When I switched to the assigned frequency I did not immediately check in. I believe the GCI site was either at DaNang or on Marble Mountain, just east of DaNang. I did not immediately transmit to ensure that the frequency was clear before transmitting. It was not. The controller was involved in directing an Air Force Phantom on several headings. Bob and I listened in fascination as we learned that the controller's unit was taken under attack by what he said were North Vietnamese helicopters. He repeated this statement several times during the course of our on station time.

The controller vectored the Air Force Phantom on a heading. The aircrew would report a contact at a range and bearing and the controller would tell him that the contact was his bandit and to shoot it down. However, the aircrew was experiencing a great amount of difficulty in keeping the target illuminated by its radar and/or locking it up.

It didn't take Bob and I long to understand that if the Air Force bird was in fact being vectored towards an enemy helicopter, it was an extremely difficult operation to get a full system lock and to actually fire a missile. The Air Force Phantoms, like the Navy Phantoms at that time, had only the pulse radar and not the Pulse Doppler radar that our squadron would be equipped with in the following deployment. As a result, looking down with the radar below the aircraft would clutter the radar scope up with so much ground return that it is extremely difficult if not impossible to see a low flying helicopter in search mode. It is more difficult to obtain a full system lock with this look down angle. Two techniques to achieve this would be to descend to an altitude below that of the helicopter and to raise the radar beam until the helicopter was illuminated by a side lobe of the radar and not the main beam.

The first option is not at all attractive at night because helicopters normally fly in the nap of the earth in a combat situation, or at exceptionally low altitude. Attempting to descend to its altitude in a Phantom at night is suicidal and would result in flying into the ground.

The second option takes a considerable amount of practice and skill to achieve and although it would permit the aircrew to illuminate the helicopter in search mode it would not assist in a full system lock because the system would have to use the main radar lobe for lock-up. When it attempted to lock-up, the excessive clutter from the ground return would "snap down" the threshold on the AGC (automatic gain control) which would cause it to lose the radar return of the helicopter and transfer lock to the ground clutter.[16]

I checked in during a rare lull in the radio traffic and was asked for our on-station time and status of our system. I replied, "state Tiger" (unrestricted) with a time on station of one hour thirty minutes and that our "gadget was sweet," ACP 165 code for up and ready. The controller then apparently ignored us for the rest of our time on station. We continued to orbit in a max conserve starboard turn and listened in fascination at the events we were witnessing.

For the next twenty minutes or so we listened to the vectors of the controller and the reply by the aircrew with no success in obtaining a firing position. At times Bob and I even had a visual on the flashing tail light of the Phantom, discernible by the heading he was flying in response to the vector ordered by GCI. It might have been a flight of two because only one, usually the wingman, will have his tail light on and flashing. We noticed that his vector took him over "feet wet" on several occasions. This was problematic because although a helicopter over land is extremely difficult to illuminate it becomes much more easily discernible over water. The return of water on the Phantom radar is almost black unless there is a high sea state which was not the case this night. Any return, yellow over a black background, is much easier to see and to obtain lock. To further compound the problem, there were several ships in the vicinity, easily seen on our radar

---

[16] There are switches to modify the clutter return and gain control but are not effective in a look down scenario in my opinion.

scopes. Ships on water provide a truly clear and distinct return to the Phantom's radar. Since we spend a considerable amount of time flying over water most Navy aircrews are very experienced in finding and discerning ships over water, so much so that an experienced aircrew can distinguish the difference between a large ship (carrier) and its supporting vessels. I used to constantly practice flying self-contained radar approaches to the carrier in the event we lost all communications and needed to return unassisted. Bob and I remarked to ourselves that we not only thought this entire evolution was strange but that most of the ships on our scopes were friendly.

After about twenty minutes (I'm writing this memoir 34 years after the fact), on yet another vector, the Air Force bird reported a contact and a lock. He was assured by the controller that the contact was his bandit and to shoot. The Air Force Phantom reported firing his missile. Shortly thereafter Bob and I heard a call on military guard frequency that a ship had been attacked by a hostile aircraft and had suffered casualties. There were several transmissions on military guard concerning the hostile fire. I believe that someone identified the ship suffering the casualty as an Australian cruiser. I may have been briefed at a later time on the ship that the vessel was a cruiser. There were several additional transmissions requesting and controlling Medevac (medical evacuation) birds for the wounded.

Bob and I believed that American forces were being attacked by North Vietnamese helicopters. The controller had stated so on several occasions. Now, a friendly ship had also been attacked by hostile forces, although even at this early time Bob and I thought it could have been friendly fire from the Air Force Phantom.

In any event, the controller continued to ignore us even though I tried several times to check in and advise him of our remaining time on station. When we reached bingo fuel we advised him that we were returning to base and switching frequencies. I don't remember him acknowledging us. We departed the area and headed for the ship. We took our assigned marshal position and completed an uneventful night recovery aboard Enterprise.

It was after midnight when we recovered aboard and since we didn't have any watches we both slept late. It wasn't until the next day that we were advised than an Australian cruiser had been hit by friendly American fire, an Air Force Phantom fired a Sparrow missile at it. I do remember reading some reports about what happened and being briefed in the ready room about how not to obtain lock on a friendly ship!

I did not think of this episode until some thirty-four years later when I began to write down my experiences in the Navy. Ross Eckert is a fellow worker at the Department of Public Safety Tucson office where I work. He is a journeyman facilities worker. In 1968 he was an Army artillery officer, a lieutenant, stationed in Chu Lai. Part of his duties involved assignment with an Army Hawk Anti-Aircraft Artillery battery. In discussing this incident with him he informed me that there was some concern that if the North Vietnamese were to use helicopters against American forces in South Vietnam it would not only be extremely difficult to locate and target them but would also be difficult to attack them successfully at night.

Ross tells me that there were many exercises conducted to test the feasibility of tracking helicopters with various Hawk search radars. The idea was to track them from one missile battery to another. He relates how there was to be a test of this capability by using American helicopters flying down Vietnam and having the Hawk battery search radars track them. He believes that this incident was one such exercise using American helicopters to test this capability and that it went terribly wrong. He believes that the area in which the GCI site was located was under attack by enemy ground forces and that the friendly exercise helicopters were assumed to be attacking and air support was requested and given by the Seventh Air Force in DaNang.

I also read from an Australian web site in which the Australian guided missile destroyer Hobart has a written description of the event. Below is a direct quote from HMAS Hobart's web site:

"Hobart returned to 'The Gun line' on 20th May 1968 for her 2nd Deployment. Straight into heavy action in 1 Corps around the DaNang vicinity saw her heading for Subic in early June for a barrel replacement for her two "5" Guns.

"Hobart returned to Sea Dragon operations on June 11th, relieving USS St Paul with Captain Shands taking command of Task Unit 77.1.2. USS Theodore Chandler (DD 717) was the support ship of the TU, which carried out its first firing on two truck parks twelve miles North of Dong Hoi.

"On 13th & 14th June both ships carried out successful firing operations around Mui Ong and Cap Lay, where both ships came under fire from coastal defense batteries, thirteen rounds landing as close as fifty yards from Hobart before she knocked out one gun and US 7th Airfoce (sic) Phantoms accounted for the remainder. Shrapnel was later collected from Hobart's upper deck. This was the third time Hobart had come under enemy fire.

"The Destroyer USS Edson had been detached from the NGFS Unit and now joined Hobart and Chandler to carry out surveillance around Tiger Island, thirteen miles east of Cap Lay where an enemy radar installation was monitoring Operation Sea Dragon. With only one extended TU in the area it was found that the garrison was being resupplied at night by sea.

"Early on the morning of June 17th Hobart detected an aircraft approaching her from the vicinity of Cap Lay and evaluated it as 'friendly'. In the meantime whilst Hobart had been trying to establish the identity of the aircraft it launched a missile which hit her amidships on the starboard side, immediately aft of the boat davit. The warhead passed through 01 Deck and penetrated the Chief Petty Officers Pantry, Radar Room 3, the Missile Director Control Room and severely damaging the Emergency Conning Platform. The body of the missile then passed through the outer skin of the after funnel, damaging its uptakes, and finished up in the forward funnel. In its passage it killed Ordinary Seaman K. D. Cramer and wounded AB Peterson and OrdSmn Swenson.

"Hobart's crew clambered to Action Stations, and three and a half minutes later another two missiles fired from close range slammed into her. Again, on the starboard side. The second missile entered her transom just below 1 Deck wrecking the Gunner's Store and Engineers Workshop, luckily the warhead did not explode. The 80 Man Aft Seamen's Mess wore a large part of this missile! The third missile hit her near the site of the first and the warhead passed through the Fan Space, Missile Director Equipment Room and No 2 Missile Director. Chief Electrician Hunt was killed and several sailors wounded by part of the missile warhead. The Ikara Missile Magazine was also seriously damaged.

"As Hobart tuned away from the threat direction the aircraft was seen to be a swept wing jet fighter. Hobart got away five rounds of "5" and no further attack was made.

"The TU joined USS Boston. And with USS Blandy DD 943 formed an anti-aircraft screen around USS Enterprise CVAN 65. A helo from Enterprise provided a medivac and delivered AB Peterson, Mech Kitterling, and AB Lee to hospital in DaNang.

"Edson relieved Hobart as leader of the TU and Hobart steamed for Subic Bay. On passage the crew cleared the debris and collected pieces of missile for identification. It was only then it was realized that the missiles had been fired from US Aircraft.

"Actually Hobart had been one of only several ships attacked by 7th Air force jets on the nights of the 16th & 17th June. On the 16th USS PCF19 was sunk near the DMZ with five killed and on the 17th Hobart, Boston and Edson were attacked. Edson 15 minutes after Hobart as were 'Market Time' vessels USCGC Point Dume WPB82325 and PCF12, a US Navy Patrol Craft. Boston and Hobart both took hits but only Hobart suffered fatalities."

Other American Naval units were also attacked at the same time. There is a link on the Hobart's web site of the American PCF (Patrol Craft Fast, or "Swift") boats, Mobile Riverine Force Association Vietnam. On this web site there is a narrative by James Steffes, who in 1968 was an Engineman Second Class (EN2) aboard PCF-12 (he is now retired, ENC). He recounts how PCF-19 was sunk by fire on that night at or slightly after midnight. In this account he states that he saw helicopters and received fire from then. I'm not sure what the official history states but one fact is that several units were attacked and struck by Air Force Phantoms firing Sparrow missiles.

"I was aboard PCF-12 on June 15, 1968, when we got underway from D Nang enroute to our assigned patrol area, Enfield Cobra Charlie. This area is off Wonder Beach South of Qua Viet. We settled into our patrol area and all seemed quiet and routine. Our crew consisted of Lt JG Pete Snyder, BM2 Johnnie P. Fitts, LPO, (myself), EN2 James Steffes, QM2 Gary Rosenberger, RD2 Jason Kenneth Block, and GMG3 Thomas Klemesh. It was our second patrol since taking over PCF-12 and it was running well.

"Around 1900 or so, we received a call from Enfield Cobra Alpha asking to meet us near the point that our patrol areas met saying they were having radar problems. The Alpha Boat was PCF-19 with LT JG John Davis's crew aboard; they were operating with a Coast Guard Cutter, the USCG Campbell. It was approximately 2000-hours when we met; it was dark when she came alongside. I hadn't been in country long and did not know the crew personally although I had seen them around the APL.

"The problem was the radar kept fading out especially at slow speeds. They could not be sure where they were and their position was critical being near the DMZ. I climbed down in the engine room with the snipe, EN2 Edward Cruz. We quickly determined that the starboard engine's alternator was not charging the bank of batteries and the radar ran off these batteries. PCF-12 had a knife switch on the after bulkhead that connected the two banks of batteries together in case of charging circuit problems. PCF-19 had no such switch and since it was not his boat he did not know where his jumper cables were, if he had any. I quickly got my set from PCF-12 and we hooked them up across the battery banks on PCF-19. Now the port engine could charge both banks of batteries. I recall chatting and laughing with my new found snipe friend, Ed Cruz as we slipped and slid in the wet bilge while hooking up these cables. With the radar working fine, we said goodbye and PCF-19 moved off in the darkness, never to be seen again.

"At approximately 0030 on June 16th, "flash traffic" was sent to all Market Time Units from the Naval Gunfire Officer at Alpha One, which is an outpost on the DMZ, part of the McNamara Line. It stated that Enfield Cobra Alpha has disappeared in a flash of light and appeared to have sunk. We proceeded at max speed to the area, arriving just as Point Dume was pulling two survivors from the water. They proceeded to Cua Viet with LTJG John Davis and GMGSN John Anderegg, both gravely wounded. After notifying CSC, Da Nang, "Article" that we were on station and assumed Enfield Cobra Alpha, we began to illuminate the area looking for survivors until we exhausted our supply of 81 MM illumination rounds. We found only debris and a fuel slick, no bodies or survivors. Suddenly, we were illuminated by four amber colored illumination rounds at a high altitude directly overhead. Mr. Snyder called Point Dume but she was still in Qua Viet. We headed south with illumination rounds continuing to light us up, following us southward. At some point, we stopped and checked our bearings. As we looked around us in the darkness with a moon that sometimes was behind clouds, we spotted two aircraft "hovering" on our port and starboard beams. They were about three hundred yards away and one hundred feet above the water. As the boat swung around to put the aircraft ahead and astern of PCF-12, I could hear Mr. Snyder requesting air support and identification of these helos. The answer from the beach was "no friendly aircraft in the area, have contacts near you on radar and starlight scope. "Are they squawking IFF?" my OIC asked. "Negative, I repeat, negative squawking IFF," came the reply.

"At this time, Mr. Snyder radioed Roger that, I am taking aircraft under fire if they show hostile intent." By this time, the helos were forward and aft of PCF-12 and I got a good look at one of the helos in the moonlight. It had a rounded front like an observation helo and it looked like two crewman sitting side by side. I went up to the pilot house to tell Mr. Snyder and standing in the doorway, I could see the other helo. I watched as tracers began to come toward us as this helo opened fire. The guns were from the nose of the helo. Our guns opened up and I ran back to my position as the loader on the after gun. We heard a crash of glass and a splash as one of the helos hit the water, the other helo broke contact and left the area.

For the next two and one half hours, we played cat and mouse with one or more helos at a time, opening up with our guns when they moved toward us in a threatening manner. We must have moved back north because we saw Point Dume nearby and blinking lights around her in the air, she was firing tracers into the air at something, but we could not see what it was. During this time, the radios were crackling constantly as my OIC answered calls from Da Nang and other units while all friendlies that could be in the area were checked out. The result was; no friendlies, these had to be North Vietnamese.

"About 0330, low on ammo, fuel and our 50 Caliber barrels burned out, PCF-12 received a call from an aircraft flight leader as they approached from the south to intercept. We were told to fire a blue flare, both us and Point Dume to mark our positions. The jets flew overhead and acknowledged our position. There were explosions and gunfire to the north as the jets looked for targets. Remember, this is at least three hours after PCf-19 went down. As dawn broke, we could only see the shoreline and the Point Dume. We went alongside a ship where we received fuel and some fifty caliber ammo. We continued to patrol and look for signs of PCF-19 until we were relieved by PCF-101 and returned to DaNang. A few days later some of our crew and some of Point Dume testified at a Board of Inquiry held at III MAF Headquarters in Da Nang.

"We continued to monitor and track these "lights" for several weeks after this up until September. In August PCF-12 and an extra crew took turns patrolling

Enfield Cobra Alpha's area for two weeks using USCG Owasco as our mother ship.

"I have pages of documents, deck logs of ships in the area, copies of mortuary logs and many more documents. I started to write a book entitled "The Sinking of PCF-19". If any of you wish to share your observations or records of that night, I will recognize you as the source of any material that I can use.

"This is my story in brief. I know what the "official story" is, but this is mine as true and complete as I can remember.

"My investigations continue to this day however not much new evidence has surfaced. Along with Larry Lail, a hospital corpsman that assisted the divers on June 16, 17, and 18 as they retrieved the bodies from the sunken PCF-19. He was aboard USS Acme, an MSO. We have located the Marine Officer on the forward most post on the beach, "Oceanview" and the Naval Gunfire Liaison Officer at Alpha One. They bear out this story as they tracked the lights for several weeks. The NGLO had a radio operator that saw the flash and explosion of PCF-19. We have also located two of the four divers, the skipper of Point Dume, the Wing Commander of the planes out of Da Nang and the pilot that was blamed for sinking PCF-19; however he has not agreed to talk to us yet."

I am sobered by reading these accounts of men who served on ships in the combat zone in direct contact with enemy forces. Although if shot down, an aircrew in a survival situation is in similar circumstance, there is always a good chance that you'll return from each mission back to the carrier where not only are you safe, but you have luxurious comforts when compared to the infantryman or sea going sailor on a small boat.

Friendly fire casualties are not only disheartening, but quite frequently can be avoided by better coordination, especially inter-service coordination. Bob and I were flying under control of an airborne FAC (forward air controller) when an Air Force Phantom delivered "short rounds" on friendly troops in South Vietnam. Neither Navy nor Air Force aircrews were trained in close air support to the extent that Marine aircrews were. During the Vietnam War, Marine crews excelled in close air support. I knew several Marines who supported friendly troops in the Ashau Valley who had to descend below a low level cloud layer between the mountains strictly on the Phantom's radar! That is another story. My assignment to JSOC in 1979 was a direct result of the failure of American Special Operations forces to conduct a joint rescue mission of American hostages in Iran. But that also is another story.

Post Script:

In 2011 I began working on my first novel 'The Shadow of Kukulkan' after a hiatus of several years. I began to write after my retirement from the Department of Public Safety on July 1, 2005. Unfortunately, Jeannie, my late wife had a stroke during her 4-hour brain surgery to remove a brain aneurysm on February 15, 2006, so for the next 5-years I was engaged full time as her caregiver and worked with her and medical personnel to get her back to some modicum of independence. Early in 2011 I again took up work on Kukulkan. The main character of the novel, Bill Castillo, was a retired Navy Chief Petty Officer who served in Swift Boats in Vietnam. I remembered this incident in which I was peripherally involved. I did some research on the internet and found a website of the Swift Sailors Association. I contacted some of the people involved in the incident including James Steffes who retired as an Engineman Chief and who authored a book about the incident entitled "Swift Boat Down.[17] They attempted for

---

[17] James Steffes, Swift Boat Down: the Real Story of the Sinking of PCF-19 (Xlibris, Bloomington, IN 2005)

years to get the official US Navy report to document action against North Vietnamese helicopters with only limited success. Although Steffes and others were awarded combat citations the US Navy today (2015) has not yet officially recognized US Navy action against North Vietnamese helicopters in June of 1968. One of the members of the Swift Boat Sailors Association was Ken Magnus, assigned as a sniper in direct support of Swift Boat crews in 1968 and who knew the individuals involved personally because he served with them. He was involved in attempting to get the Navy to set the record straight and struck up some correspondence with me via email and phone calls. I was impressed with his efforts and volunteered to write a letter to Senator McCain (Arizona). In the process I became familiar with quite a bit of historical documentation involving the incident but was unable to find the CINCLANT Final Report of the Board of Inquiry that took place, only the Interim Report which is inconclusive. I've attached my letter to McCain and a copy of CINCLANT's Interim Report as an Appendix to this chapter.

APPENDIX A TO CHAPTER 11

May 11, 2011

The Honorable John S. McCain

241 Russell Senate Office Building
United States Senate
Washington, DC 20510

Enclosure (1) Officer in Charge (OINC) of US Navy
PCF-12 After Action Report dated June 24, 1968

Enclosure (2) US Navy Office of Chief of Naval
Operations letter 5752 dated November 10, 2009

Enclosure (3) Department of the Air Force Office of
Legislative Liaison letter dated June 25, 2010

Enclosure (4) USS Boston (CAG1) Deck Log Sunday,
June 16, 1968

Dear Senator McCain:

I am requesting your assistance in correcting an error and
omission in the record of United States Military Combat
Operations in Vietnam which occurred on June 16, 1968.
This action involved US Navy Swift Boats in battle
against North Vietnamese Helicopters and involved many
individuals and units including American and Allied
forces. This incident was the first of many subsequent
incidents which followed in the hours and days after the
initial battle and is misstated in the historical record as a
result of its rapid tempo of operations, multiple incidents
involved, and the numerous personnel and units which
participated. What occurred can be attributed inter alia to
the "Fog of War" which often occurs in battle.

Enclosure (1), the After Action Report submitted by the Officer in Charge of PCF-12 (Patrol Craft Fast) is the most salient document in the record of what occurred. It was not given due consideration in the numerous reports and investigations which followed the series of events subsequent to the initial battle.

For the crews of the United States Navy Swift Boats that were involved, the survivors, those killed in action and those wounded in action, and their families, the wait to set the record straight has already taken 43 years with no apparent hope of doing so in sight. That is why I am requesting your assistance. Both the Air Force and Navy have recommended congressional assistance in this endeavor.

Following is a brief summary of what occurred that night:

At approximately 0030H (Local Time) on June 16, 1968, a United States Navy Swift Boat, PCF- 19 (Patrol Craft Fast), was sunk by enemy fire off the northern coast of South Vietnam in waters to the east of the Demilitarized Zone between North and South Vietnam. Swift Boat PCF-12 was ordered to immediately proceed to the area to conduct rescue operations. When she arrived an American ship, the US Coast Guard Cutter (USCGC) Point Dume (WPB-82325), was already on station and had picked up two wounded survivors and departed the area for Cua Viet to obtain medical care for them.

After PCF-12 arrived she began to illuminate the area with green illumination rounds but was unsuccessful in finding survivors: only oil slick and debris from the sunken patrol craft. The Swift Boat began to be illuminated by amber appearing high altitude illumination rounds from an unidentified source. At this point PCF-12 headed to the south and the illumination rounds continue to follow her. At some point in time

117

PCF-12 stopped to obtain its bearings. At this time, the crew observed two hovering aircraft from above which were visually identified as hovering helicopters. The Skipper of PCF-12 contacted supporting forces to determine if these helicopters were friendly and was advised there were no friendly aircraft in his vicinity. The two enemy helicopters positioned themselves on either side of PCF-12. Shortly thereafter the Swift Boat was taken under fire by a helicopter's forward mounted chin gun and by rocket attack. The tracers were visible from the helicopter to the vicinity of the Swift Boat and observed by the crew. The Skipper of PCF-12 skillfully maneuvered his boat placing one of the helicopters directly off his bow and the other directly astern to achieve the best possible position to return fire placing both of his 50-caliber guns in optimum firing position. Several crew members observed a hit on the adversary accompanied by the sound of breaking glass and a loud splash as the enemy helicopter struck the water.

After this firefight PCF-12 joined with the USGC Point Dume who had returned to her assigned station and was also firing at the helicopters that could be seen by the blinking red lights they displayed.

North Vietnamese helicopters had sunk PCF-19, had attacked PCF-12 and Point Dume and had suffered one loss in the battle.

The battle was accompanied by extensive radio traffic and US Air Force Fighters were scrambled from the Air Base at Da Nang. Two of these fighters flew by PCF-12 and the Point Dume three hours or so later which complied with the request to display blue identification illumination rounds to mark them as friendly. These Air Force Phantoms were enroute in an attempt to locate and attack the helicopters.

The next night, on June 17, 1968, an Air Force Fighter, a Phantom F4, struck the Australian Cruiser

HMAS Hobart with its air to air missile, a Sparrow, causing damage and casualties to the ship, including killed in action.

Because of the rapid sequence of events, the hostile action taken by North Vietnamese helicopters against the Swift Boats was mistakenly included in the friendly fire incidents subsequent to the original battle as a result of investigations into the matter. As a result of that confusion, the attacks on the two Swift Boats on the night of June 16, 1968, were mistakenly included in the list of friendly fire incidents including the one involving HMAS Hobart which occurred on June 17, 1968. The later investigation also determined that there were no hostile helicopters involved and that PCF-19 had been sunk by US Air Force fighters and had attacked PCF-12! It is this egregious error that has resulted in the mistake of confusing enemy hostile action against PCF-19 and PCF-12 with that of the friendly fire against HMAS Hobart 24 hours or so later.

I have been advised that the Weapon System Officer involved in the mistakenly designated friendly fire PCF-19 attack was court martialed. He was not involved in a friendly fire attack. PCF-19 was sunk by enemy action! If he did receive disciplinary action in this matter an injustice has been done.

This error was made from an incomplete investigation and a mistaken conclusion from the facts made available to the investigating boards convened by Military authority. However, the most salient witnesses to the event, the men of the Swift Boats who were engaged in the battle, either were not consulted thoroughly or were not given credibility or were ignored in their reports of what happened.

To this date, those killed in action, wounded in action, all the participants of that battle, have failed to receive proper recognition for their engagement in this firefight with units of the North Vietnamese Military. The list of names of all those involved are included in Tab A.

I have included documents supporting the facts of what occurred that night. One of the major facts that any impartial reviewer of these documents should conclude is that the Skipper and crew of PCF-12 acquitted themselves gallantly and with valor in battle against this hostile force and shot down one of the attacking helicopters. Yet, because of the erroneous findings of the subsequent investigations they have not received the recognition that courage and merit in battle warrants.

I respectfully request that you or your staff thoroughly review the documents included with this letter request to determine what actually occurred. The Navy has documented its willingness to correct the record (Enclosure 2) but the Air Force has been unable to do so for a variety of reasons which are listed in the enclosed documents (Enclosure 3).

Enclosure (4) is a copy of the Deck Log of the USS Boston also included in Jim Steffe's book, "Swift Boat Down". All of the Enclosures are in this book. The Officer of the Deck (OOD) states in the Deck Log that at "... 0010 received three rounds of hostile fire. Evaluated probable rockets, source unknown." This action occurred just before PCF-19 was hit. The OOD made this evaluation based on his experience of combat operations. The Commanding Officer personally took the "conn" (control) of the ship from the OOD indicating his tactical decision to defend the ship from hostile threat. This entry gives further credence that PCF-19 was struck by hostile rockets and not friendly fire air-to-air missiles. The Deck Log further states: "0305 sounded General Quarters when Navy small craft was taken under fire two miles off port beam by enemy helicopter." The Deck Log of a US Navy vessel is a legal document and this one still remains unchanged.

I respectfully request that you ask the Navy to reclassify the sinking of PCF-19 and subsequent attack on PCF-12 by North Vietnamese helicopters as hostile action to correct the record.

I respectfully request that you ask the Air Force to expend all effort in due diligence to obtain, declassify and release the pertinent document(s) that proves PCF-19 was sunk by enemy action and not friendly fire.

Some of the surviving crew members believe that the reasons the Air Force may be reluctant to vigorously support clarification of the record is due to embarrassment of the friendly fire incidents. There is also a belief among some of the participants that the Air Force may have undertaken efforts with the Navy to raise the North Vietnamese helicopter lost in the battle because it has been identified as a Russian built MI-8 helicopter flown by the NVAF (North Vietnamese Air Force) and included a Russian 'advisor' who was killed in the incident. The MI-8 was a state of the art helicopter in 1968 and the US would have likely expended a great deal of effort to recover it and exploit any new or effective Soviet technology it contained. Many members believe that in order to prevent compromise of this operation the Air Force used a cover story of friendly fire to deflect unwarranted interest from the media or hostile intelligence services or both. You will see from reviewing the documents listed in the book that many were originally classified 'SECRET' and 'NO FORN.' Highly classified documents are not readily available to those seeking to determine the facts of what happened and to correct any mistakes in the historical record.

After 43 years since the battle, this classification is no longer required.

US Navy divers confirmed that PCF-19 was sunk by rockets. It is highly likely that responding US Air Force Phantoms were not armed with rockets but were armed with air-to-air missiles which were involved in the incidents of friendly fire. There is evidence only of enemy munitions involved with PCF-19 and none of US munitions.

I have included a list of those participants who are still alive and who have been active in attempting to correct the historical record, together with their addresses, phone numbers and email to assist your staff in contacting them directly at Tab B. They have extensive knowledge of the events in question and also extensive experience in attempting to get the Air Force to cooperate fully with them.

I was only a peripheral participant to the events subsequent to the sinking of PCF-19 and the attack on PCF-12. I was a US Navy Radar Intercept Officer (RIO) assigned to Fighter Squadron Ninety Six embarked on USS Enterprise (CVAN 65) that June in 1968. My pilot and I were diverted from a scheduled Armed Reconnaissance mission over North Vietnam to assist Air Force Air Controllers in the area in their attempt to locate and destroy hostile North Vietnamese helicopters. I was airborne when HMAS Hobart was struck by friendly fire and heard her calls on Military Guard Frequency for assistance and MedEvac. The Air Force air controller had no need of our services that night and after we reached the minimum fuel state requirement for mission termination we returned to the Enterprise.

However, years later in seeking to determine what actually occurred that night I discovered the men of the units involved through the internet and after learning that they had been unsuccessful in reclassifying the attacks on PCF-19 and PCF-12 from friendly fire to hostile action volunteered to assist by offering to write this letter request to you, Senator McCain, since I am one of your constituents and you are my Senator as well as a retired US Navy officer who served in Vietnam.

I have included in the attached documents a book written by one of the participants, James Steffes, who was an Engineman Second Class Petty Officer aboard PCF-12 and who had visited the crew of PCF-19 just prior to the battle and its loss. James Steffes retired from the US Navy as a Chief Engineman and authored a book about the incident titled "Swift Boat Down." It offers compelling evidence that PCF-19 and 12 were attacked by North Vietnamese helicopters. I also strongly recommend you review the Combat After Action report dated June 24, 1968 (Enclosure 1) submitted by Lieutenant Junior Grade Pete Snyder, the Officer-in-Charge of PCF-12. It is my observation that his Combat After Action Report should have been considered by the Board of Investigation that looked into the incident as one of the most salient eyewitness accounts of the battle but it appears to me that it has not been given due recognition.

I thank you in advance for any assistance you may provide to these fellow Americans and Shipmates who have served their country well in setting the record straight: not only for their benefit but for the Nation's as well.

Very respectfully,

Eugene L. Sierras, Jr., CDR USN (RET)

Attachments:[18]

---

[18] I have chosen not to list the name of those involved to protect their privacy.

CHAPTER TWELVE

Board Of Inquiry

In January 1969, Enterprise entered Pearl Harbor, Hawaii, enroute to a WestPac deployment off of North Vietnam. All hands were manning the rail in Tropical Dress Whites. I was on deck with several of my friends in the squadron. My Line Division was also nearby on the port side. As Enterprise began to pass the USS ARIZONA Memorial she rendered honors to that sunken but proud old battleship. The call came booming over the 1MC:

"On deck attention to port! Hand salute!"

We held our salute for just a minute or so as we passed abeam the memorial.

"Ready, two! Carry on. Carry on."

Little was I to know that in a matter of days I would come as close to death as I ever came in the Navy.

In January 1969, I had one WestPac combat cruise under my belt. I was proficient and confident not only in my abilities, which had been tested in battle, but in the magnificent war bird which took me into harm's way and back again, ever reliable, ever steady. VF96 transitioned from the F4B to the F4J. The birds the squadron received were new, recently off the production line at St. Louis. Each contained the most updated ECM gear available. The radar was the AWG10, which had Pulse Doppler. These warbirds were truly a pleasure to fly. The aircraft we received were never assigned to another squadron but had come to us directly from the acceptance trials and modification.

The F4J was truly an all-weather fighter-interceptor-attack platform, limited in capability only by the crew. Like every other squadron, about half of the junior officers (Lieutenant and below) were new, either directly from the RAG on their first tour or returning to the fleet after a shore duty tour. The remainder, like me, was on their second deployment with their first assigned squadron. The senior officers were all combat experienced, although for some, this was their first tour in the Phantom. All of us participated on the training cycle which started with single ship "familiarization" flights and ended with a coordinated ship/Air Wing Operational Readiness Exercise. While in Pearl Harbor, we were scheduled to conduct our Operational Readiness Inspection which would certify us for combat in WestPac.

I was assigned to fly with LT CDR Ernie Mares, an ex-A4 pilot. Like many previous single-seat pilots, Earnie was skeptical about sharing duties with another crewman until he flew in the high intensity, high threat environment over North Vietnam.

North Vietnam, in 1969, possessed a highly sophisticated and deadly Air Order of Battle. The Soviet Union equipped the North Vietnamese with the latest in Soviet weaponry, technology, and tactics. Although never explicitly stated in writing, we knew that Soviet "advisors" took an active role in combat, including manning the SAM missile batteries and flying MiG aircraft. In was not too farfetched to consider North Vietnam a testing and proving ground for a larger, non-nuclear, air-war in Europe. In this high threat environment, a single seat pilot could be overwhelmed by the demands of penetrating enemy airspace, taking evasive action against SAM missiles, anti-aircraft artillery, and MiGs, while maintaining visual formation with friendly aircraft, navigating to a target, prosecuting a successful attack, and egressing successfully. Ernie came to appreciate the two-man crew concept.

After the ship tied up I visited the Line Division Office to talk to the Chief, First Class, other Petty Officers, and the division about liberty on the beach. The watch bill reviewed and implemented and all was in good order. I was proud of my division and of the Chief. The loading aboard the aircraft in Alameda prior to deployment was flawless and I received a compliment from the Maintenance Officer, Lieutenant Commander John Disher (later Admiral Disher) that he had never seen such a trouble free evolution. I readily acknowledged to John that the success of the loading was due to the Chief and First Class Aviation Boatswains Mate Martineau who supervised it. They were both experienced and successfully completed a first class job.

John Disher reminded me when I was assigned as Line Division Officer he asked me if I would consider taking the Chief. Chief Petty Officer Smith (not his real name) was returned to the fleet after a period of alcohol rehabilitation. He struggled with alcoholism for several years resulting in a steady degradation of his performance. The Navy permitted him a final chance by the Navy to successfully complete his rehabilitation and remain free of alcohol or be discharged from the Navy prior to his twenty year retirement eligibility. Several of the other division officers in the department refused to take him. I reviewed the Chief's personnel jacket prior to making my decision and determined I would take a chance on him. He had a sterling record until he began to encounter problems with alcohol. Two factors assisted me in my decision. The first was that I was not experienced in the Maintenance Department. Most Lieutenants already served several assignments. I did not (I was previously a surface officer). The second factor was that the Leading Petty Officer, Petty Officer First Class, was Martineau who could take the Chief's responsibility if necessary. It didn't appear that I would be assigned a Chief Petty Officer if I didn't accept Smith. Martineau discussed this with me and advised me that other Chief Petty Officers in the squadron ostracized Chief Smith "somewhat" and that he needed this chance to prove himself. Martineau believed in him and so did I. My decision turned out to be a good one. Chief Petty Officer Smith more than proved himself to me, the Navy, and to himself. Petty Officer Martineau would be dead in a matter of days after we entered Pearl Harbor.

This was not my first visit to Hawaii. I accompanied a few of my squadron mates, visiting some of the normal tourist attractions, visiting the Memorial, the beaches and heading into town to visit the local watering holes. My energies were focused more on the upcoming deployment to Vietnam.

The ship and Air Wing were scheduled for an Operational Readiness Inspection (ORI) after our three day visit. This was a full battle-dress rehearsal which would determine how combat-ready we were. The morning we stood out of Pearl Harbor for the ORI I was busy ensuring the Line Division was ready for the inspection. Everything from personnel training and qualification records to observation of operating procedures of my Division were to be observed and graded by the inspectors. I experienced several inspections as a surface officer but this was my first in the Maintenance Department and I wanted everything to go well. The Line Division was divided into two branches: Plane Captains and Troubleshooters.

Plane Captains were those sailors responsible for the care, cleaning and pre-flight readiness of the aircraft. They underwent a rigorous training and qualification program and not every candidate was successful. They were junior enlisted, mostly non-rated, Airman or Airman Apprentice. After a successful tour as plane captain and promotion they would be transferred into another Maintenance branch where they would work in their rating. Aboard ship each Plane Captain lived almost twenty-four hours a day with his aircraft. His name was stenciled on his assigned aircraft along with those of the pilot and RIO. They took considerable pride in what they considered "their aircraft." I was confident my plane captains would do well. They had been operating together now for about six-months, with about one month at sea. Although still settling down into a routine, I observed them in action around the clock during flight operations and knew they were ready for the expected rigorous flight operations and ORI.

The training and qualification records were also in excellent shape, accurate and completely reflecting each individual's training and qualification. Both the Chief and Petty Officer Martineau were highly experienced and knowledgeable. I reviewed each record with the two of them in great detail and knew we were in good shape. This fact would become especially important to me later.

The Troubleshooter branch was in even better shape. Troubleshooters were experienced Petty Officers, Third Class to First Class, but normally Second Class, which conducted final pre-flight inspections and last minute checks of the aircraft when on the catapult seconds prior to launch. They possessed authority to signal thumbs-up or thumbs-down to the Catapult Officer to indicate

127

whether an aircraft was ready for launch or was to be taken off the catapult and returned to the line for further maintenance. They were given this consequential authority because they were assigned significant responsibility for the safety of the aircraft before it was catapulted off the ship, accelerating from zero to one hundred fifty knots in less than two and a half-seconds. They were nominated to serve as Troubleshooters by each maintenance branch officer with the recommendation and approval of the Work Center Supervisor, or Leading Petty Officer of the branch.

Both the Troubleshooters and Plane Captains were required to pass an oral board of the squadron's officers who were stakeholders in their performance. Needless to say, they represented the cream of the crop and I was not only confident in their abilities but proud to lead them.

I was eager and ready for the Inspection. I felt refreshed after a good night's sleep. Ernie and I were scheduled for the first launch. We would be carrying six five hundred pound general purpose bombs and two five inch Zuni rocket pods on each wing, together with two Sparrow and two Sidewinder missiles. We were schedule to participate in a coordinated strike against a target designated at sea.

Briefing was thorough and conducted via the ship's closed-circuit television system to each ready room. After briefing Ernie and I suited up and proceeded to the flight deck where we greeted our plane captain and Petty Officer Martineau. Pre-flight inspection and start-up were normal. Our aircraft was spotted, or parked, on the rear starboard quarter of the flight deck, just forward of the fantail. There were several other Phantoms and Corsairs (A7) parked just aft of us on the fan tail, lined up from starboard to port. After we completed our start-up and engine-checks we waited for our turn to taxi forward to the catapult. We were to be launched early in the sequence, about the fifth or sixth birds, after the BARCAP and tankers. Our canopies were closed and all systems were up and ready.

I remember watching a flight deck director (yellow shirt) approach our aircraft and rendering to Ernie and the plane captain the hand signal for "hold brakes," "remove tie down chains." At that time I bent over to make a final adjustment of my navigation computer. As I was entering the updated coordinates I felt the aircraft carrier shudder and heard what sounded like a muted thump against our aircraft. I immediately looked up and tried to look out the canopy. I couldn't see anything because the canopy was opaque, rendered so by fuel which had been splattered against the canopy. As I gazed at the canopy I saw the fuel ran down the canopy enough for me to see the flight deck. I was shocked by what I saw. There were several people lying on the flight deck. Several aircraft were on fire. I still vividly remember the bright orange flames and black smoke across the flight deck. I didn't know exactly what happened but I instantaneously knew that a catastrophe had occurred and that I only had seconds to decide which would determine if I lived or died. I read the extensive after-action reports on fires which occurred on the USS Oriskany and the USS Forrestal. I knew what from the reports what caused those fires, but more importantly, I knew that several people died by not making quick decisions to act.

I made the decision to eject. I flipped down the alternate ejection handle guard and grabbed the alternate ejection handle between my legs. At that time I heard the engines of our aircraft winding down and saw the "canopy open" light on the warning panel. Ernie shut down the engines and opened his canopy. I believed that if I ejected with his canopy open the rocket blast from my H-7 seat could kill or injure him. (I would later learn that this was not the case.) I immediately flipped the alternate ejection handle guard back into position, popped open my canopy, pulled the emergency oxygen disconnect handle on the left side of my seat while I simultaneously pulled the emergency exit handle on the right side of the ejection seat. This released the oxygen hose to my mask and cut the leg straps around my legs and released the harness locks to the seat. I immediately exited the aircraft over the right canopy sill because I witnessed the flames and smoke increasing in intensity to the port side.

Normal egress from the canopy is from the port side by stepping onto the top of the intake, then moving sideways to the front canopy, then stepping down the ladder which is released by a button on the aircraft exit step. I went over the starboard side jumping from the starboard-intake directly down onto the flight deck, a drop of some six feet. Why didn't I break a leg or ankle with sixty pounds of flight gear strapped to me I don't know unless I was so pumped with adrenalin that I had more than normal strength. (I would later turn in the oxygen "middle-block" to the airframes shop with the yellow metal handle extended beyond its normal length by about four inches!)

I remember running from the spot where I landed on the flightdeck to the edge then leaping onto the "catwalk," again, a drop of about five-feet. This evolution was in "slow motion." I knew that I only experienced the first of more explosions to come and that if the next one came while I was on the flight deck it would probably kill me, blow me over the side into the water, or both. As soon as I landed on the catwalk a second explosion occurred again shaking the entire ship.

I remember a sailor in a white T-shirt with no hat standing in the catwalk looking out at the events transpiring. His eyes were wide open and he was in some type of shock. I hollered at him to follow me as I left the catwalk and entered the ship. There was a tall Chief Petty Officer standing in the passageway directing traffic to the forward part of the ship, away from the stern. The sailor and I made our way forward. I eventually made it back to the Ready Room where I took off my gear and watched the crew fight the fire through the ship's television circuit. There are several openings on the flight deck where cameras are located. One can get a flight deck perspective. There are also several cameras mounted on the superstructure in the vicinity of "PriFly," which can provide several views of the flight deck from above. The ship's crew was piping the images from these cameras into the ship's system. The Ready Room had a monitor so we could watch real time events.

I remember seeing the flight deck crew manning hoses and moving as an organized crew to the conflagration taking place. Then there would be a white out of the camera signifying an explosion. When the television screen cleared we could see the crew running from the area with aircraft parts raining down on them and onto the flight deck. We witnessed seeing several people lying prostrate on the flight deck after each explosion. After each explosion, the flight deck crew would again man the hoses and approach the fire in an organized, highly effective manner, fighting the fire. Another explosion would occur, and the events would repeat. The crew, through their heroic and gallant efforts, persevered and won the fight, probably saving the ship.

After I took my flight gear off and spent a few minutes watching the camera in the Ready Room, I made my way onto the catwalk on the port side, forward of the waist catapults. I could see that the plane guard destroyer, USS Rogers DD 876, was immediately adjacent to the carrier on the rear port quarter where the conflagration was raging. The Destroyer Skipper maneuvered his ship so close to the carrier that there was only an exceedingly small separation between the two vessels. The destroyer's crew was manning a fire nozzle on the superstructure and pouring water from the ship onto the carrier's flight deck. Each explosion knocked down and injured some of the crew but they would be immediately replaced by others to man the nozzle and keep a steady stream of water flowing onto the flight deck. I am still awed to this day by the heroism of that Skipper and his crew.

From that point in time until the fire was successfully fought and extinguished, I don't remember what I did or where I went. After the fire was quenched and as soon as I could I made my way to the "Line Shack," or the compartment immediately under the flight deck where my Line Division office was. The Chief met me with tears in his eyes to tell me that six men from the Division had been killed, including Aviation Boatswain's Mate First Class Martineau, and that six were severely burned and medically evacuated off the ship by helicopter to Tripler Army Hospital in Honolulu.

Three others in VF 96 also lost their lives on that day. One flight crew, pilot and RIO, LT JG Don Anderson and LT JG Buddy Pyeatt, and the Aviation Ordnance Officer, LT JG Carl Bergholt, who was under the aircraft that started the fire. One of my plane captains saved the life of Air Force CAPT Jack Heffernan who when exiting the aircraft became entangled in his parachute harness and was hanging over the side of the aircraft. The plane captain came to his aid and either cut the harness to release him or lifted him up enough to take the slack off the harness to allow Jack to release them.

A total of twenty-seven men died that day on Enterprise, not to mention those who were injured and/or burned. After the fire was out the ship stood down from General Quarters. Billy Boatwright and I toured the flight deck. There was a large gaping hole in the flight deck under which there was a head (bathroom). Several of the ship's crew in the head were killed.

I walked over to where my aircraft was located. There was not much left of it, a few solid pieces, most no bigger than a couple of yards, and a pile of melted and fused ashes. Had I not exited the aircraft in good time that would have been my funeral pyre.

One of my Troubleshooters, Aviation Metalsmith (Air Frames) Second Class Smith (not his real name) was not yet medically evacuated off the ship to the Tripler Army Hospital Burn-Center in Honolulu. He was scheduled to be airlifted to the Air Force Burn Center in San Antonio, Texas. Several other burn victims were previously airlifted. After the ship tied up to the pier I requested permission from the Skipper, CDR C. E. Myers, to leave the ship with a military vehicle to visit him. I quickly received permission. I visited him daily for five days until he was airlifted to San Antonio. Petty Officer Smith was a big, strong man. He was black and was one of my best and most respected Troubleshooters. His knowledge, skill and professionalism were some of the reasons he was nominated and accepted by the board for Troubleshooter. He was also a courageous man. Severely burned over a large portion of his body, he was in obvious pain. He was not able to lie in any position on his hospital bed without enduring severe discomfort. His morale was high. He was glad to see me and appreciated my daily visits to him. He told me that as severely as he was burned he was thankful to be alive and he intended to make a complete recovery and would continue his career in the United States Navy.

When I went to visit him I passed through a ward in which I estimated there was a hundred or more young men who although they suffered different wounds, all shared one thing in common. They all suffered wounds to their face which required reconstructive surgery to their nose. Everyone wore a bandage and one or two hoses in their nose. The average age was about twenty years. I remember walking through their ward every day and greeting them and being greeted by them. No one seemed other than in good spirits. I suppose that other than their facial wounds they were either not severely injured or had recovered sufficiently to be placed in this ward.

The extent of the cost of the Vietnamese War was obvious to me as I entered and passed through this ward daily. I still remember graphically to this day the faces of those young men and their eyes looking at me, all with bandages on their nose and tubes running into and from them.

The last day I visited Petty Officer Smith he told me he was scheduled to leave for San Antonio later that day. I wished him well and thanked him for what he did. We promised each other that we would stay connected but I never heard from him again. I'm sure he needed to devote all his energy to the surgeries he faced and the rehabilitation that followed in order to continue on with his career and life. I have always thought of him, and the others who were burned or died that day. I wish them well and hope they had a good life.

Billy and I both thought that the extensive damage Enterprise suffered meant that we would return to CONUS (continental United States) for repairs. We also knew that the carrier was scheduled for a yard period late summer of 1969 which meant she couldn't be extended on her tour beyond that date. We knew that the yard period involved reworking her nuclear fuel so it was not something that could be rescheduled. We were both almost certain that we would be going home. At worse, we figured we would be transferred to other squadrons on other ships. VF 96 lost six aircraft in the fire, which was fifty percent of our complement, so we figured that was an additional reason for returning home. We were wrong. The Navy decided to repair Enterprise in Pearl Harbor. Shipyard workers rallied to her plight volunteering to work extra hours and even off duty to repair the ship and send her back to war. This was a tradition since Yorktown arrived damaged from the battle of Coral Sea and needed expeditious repairs for the upcoming battle of Midway during World War II. Yorktown was repaired in about a month's time with workers still doing repairs on her as she stood out of Pearl Harbor to face the Japanese at Midway.

The end result was that Enterprise was made whole again, fully repaired, and an exact month after the accident stood out of Pearl

Harbor on her way to WestPac for another combat tour off Vietnam. VF 96 received six additional replacement F4J birds, not directly off the production line like those lost, but from other squadrons.

Chief Smith and I reformed the Line Division and Troubleshooter branch and we were again fully operational. Needless to say, all hands were particularly aware of the safety requirements of our job.

After the fire, the Navy formed a Board of Inquiry to determine the cause of the incident and to recommend corrective action to ensure it wouldn't happen again. Enterprise was the third carrier to experience devastating fires and the Navy was determined to ensure it would not happen again.

After the fire VF96 and our sister squadron, VF92, were moved ashore to operate out of Kaneohe Marine Corps Air Station. We received our replacement aircraft, reformed our squadron, and flew extensive training missions while ashore to keep our proficiency at combat ready status.

I received orders to report to the Board of Inquiry with my personnel training records. The Board was chaired by a two star admiral and was convened aboard Enterprise. I had never been closer to an admiral than in ranks at inspection or in the audience at an auditorium to hear an address. Needless to say, I was concerned. The Uniform of the Day was Tropical Khaki Long. In those days, which was without ribbons. I paid meticulous attention to my uniform. I already wore my hair high and tight but I got a fresh haircut just to be sure. I gathered all my Division's training records including both those of the plane captains and the Troubleshooters and went over them with the Chief to ensure they were complete. I was careful to ensure no new entries were made. I wanted to deliver them to the Board the way they were the day of the fire. I then spent several hours with them in my state room going over them until I could almost recite from memory all the qualifications, standards, and evaluations of each man's record. I was prepared to discuss them at great length in front of the Board and believed I could answer any question I was asked.

I reported early and announced my name and rank to the Marine sentry who entered into a compartment for a minute then returned and told me to enter. Since I was covered, even though aboard ship, the sentry saluted me and I returned his salute as I entered the compartment. There was a Navy Lieutenant who greeted me. Since he was uncovered I removed my cover. He asked if I brought the training records and I told him yes. He asked to see them and then took them from me, told me to have a seat until I was called, and disappeared into the compartment that I assumed was the hearing room.

I was seated for about twenty minutes when the LT returned and told me to enter the hearing room. He motioned for me to take position at the end of a long table, covered with a standard Navy issue green felt table cloth. I noticed everyone had an ashtray at their seat but me. I walked to the end of the table, came to attention and announced, "LT Eugene Sierras, reporting as ordered, Sir." I was conscious of all the Board members, who were seated, looking at me, except the admiral who was either making notes or reading something in front of him. After only a few seconds he looked at me, acknowledged my presence, and asked, or actually ordered, me to be seated. I sat down with my back erect. If it was possible to sit at attention, I was doing it. I expected to be sworn in, something similar to, do you agree to tell the truth, the whole truth, and nothing but the truth? That didn't happen.

The LT then took position standing next to the Admiral. He said "LT Sierras is the VF96 Line Division Officer. Six of his men were killed during the fire and six have been medically evacuated to the San Antonio Burn Center for severe burns."

The admiral acknowledged his statement and glanced around at the other Board members, the most junior of which was a full Commander. They asked me several questions about my Division's training and qualification procedures for plane captains and Troubleshooters. I was aware these officers, aviators all, were at least as familiar, if not more familiar with the procedures, than I. I answered their few questions. They had my records before them I noticed and had been reviewing them before I entered the room and continued to do so while I was there.

Nothing was said for a few minutes until the LT said, "LT Sierras was also involved in the fire. He was in an F4 that was completely burned to the deck. There was nothing left of it but a pile of ashes."

I watched the admiral as he looked up at me. Although the somber expression on his face didn't change, I could see an acknowledgment of something in his eyes, which, although I could not ascertain exactly what it was, I knew, bore me no ill will. In fact, it seemed to me to be an understanding of my recent peril from someone who also experienced peril. If there wasn't kindness in his eyes it was certainly something remarkably close to it.

He nodded and said to me, "LT Sierras thank you for coming today. I wish you well. That is all."

I looked at the LT who nodded. I stood up, came to attention, did an about face and exited the space.

I received my training records in two weeks. I never heard from the Board again, nor did I ever read its official report although the entire squadron and ship, indeed, the entire Navy, learned of its findings.

Human error caused the tragedy aboard Enterprise. I learned as a boot Seaman Recruit that the Navy's safety regulations were written in blood by the hard experience of others. This was true in Enterprise's case.

Navy aircraft are started by small jet engines contained in a mobile vehicle called a "tractor." The tractors are mobile, necessary to move from aircraft to aircraft. The tractor used by the F4 aboard ship and ashore was designated "MD3". The MD3 has a hose from an outlet that when fitted to the aircraft opening beneath the engine would send high pressure air into the engine, striking the engine blades and rotating them until, at a certain percent of engine RPM, the pilot would advance the throttle sending atomized fuel into the burner cans and press the igniter which causes the atomized fuel to burn further turning the engine until it achieved idle RPM.

The tractor has an exhaust for the small jet engine. The temperature of the engine exhaust is 1200-degrees Centigrade up to twelve inches away from the exhaust opening on the tractor. The tractor used to start the VF 96 F4 which caused the fire contained a hole or opening in a section of the starter hose. It was sent to maintenance for repair but rather than replacing the starter hose the hose was shortened to eliminate that portion of it with the hole. As a result the hose was not long enough to properly position the tractor to ensure that the exhaust would not impinge on the aircraft or the ordnance carried by the aircraft. This forced the tractor driver to park too close to the aircraft and position the exhaust so that it impinged on the Zuni five inch rocket pod carried on the port wing of the F4. The hot exhaust caused the warhead on the Zuni rocket to explode low order (not with the full explosive force of the warhead which would have killed everyone in a wide area around the aircraft) and which ruptured the six hundred gallon centerline fuel tank carried by the F4. The fuel from the ruptured tank spilled onto the flight deck where it was ignited (either by the tractor's exhaust or by the burning rocket or both) and caused the fire to rapidly expand, exploding additional warheads and rupturing additional fuel tanks. In a brief time a conflagration was raging on Enterprise's flight deck.

The plane captain of the aircraft involved saw the Zuni rocket warhead turning color from white to reddish pink and tried to advise someone of what was occurring. He was unable to do so and left the area which saved his life. He was the plane captain that later helped CAPT Jack Heffernan disentangle from his parachute harness while hanging over the side of his aircraft, thus saving his life as well.

One good experience my room mate, Billy Boatwright and I underwent, was to bring our wives over from the states and spend five weeks in a beach bungalow at Camp Bellows Air Force Station. Juley brought my son Eddy over and Billy's wife brought her children over as well. There was enough time after our duty and flying days to be tourists and enjoy the sights of Hawaii.

Enterprise and VF 96 steamed out of Pearl Harbor en route to Vietnam. However, a year after the Pueblo was captured by the North Koreans, a Navy EC121 reconnaissance aircraft was shot down by the North Korean Air Force. Enterprise was again ordered to the waters off Korea to standby for action against the North Koreans. Again, we spent a month flying in cold, miserable weather conditions. The United States did not take punitive military action in this incident. At least this time we had the cold weather exposure suits aboard.

After a month in Korean waters Enterprise again steamed for the warmer waters of the South China Sea and completed another combat cruise on Yankee Station. The Line Division not only performed their task well but became one of the best in the Air Wing. I received the Navy Achievement Medal in part for helping to reform and lead the Line Division which achieved a sustained excellence after the fire. I accepted the Medal but it was truly a reflection of the work the Chief did, as well as that of the petty officers and men in the Division. The Chief received an award for his contributions and was welcomed back into the Chief Petty Officer community in the squadron as a respected member. He went on to retire at the end of the cruise. I believe he was proud of his tour in VF 96. Petty Officer Martineau lives in my memories of that time.

US Navy photo of Enterprise aft of the starboard stern looking at damage.

Photo of USS Rogers alongside Enterprise assisting in firefighting; there were several explosions which occurred causing casualties among the personnel that were manning the fire hoses. They were immediately replaced by others. The firefighting crews of both ships displayed extraordinary heroism.

CHAPTER THIRTEEN

Soar Like An Eagle

THE GREAT MAJORITY OF MY MISSIONS IN VIETNAM WERE AIR-TO-AIR which included the BARCAP, MIGCAP, and TARCAP missions. The remainder were strike missions carrying air-to-ground ordnance against enemy targets in North Vietnam. There were occasional air-to-ground sorties over South Vietnam, always under control of a FAC[19]. We were not trained in Close Air Support missions which required extremely demanding coordination in laying down ordnance in support of friendly troops.

I served with Marine Aircrews who are among the best trained in the world in close air support and respect their ability. I learned of missions in which Marine F4 aircrews laid down Snake and 'Nape[20] parallel to Marines less than 50 meters from friendly positions. Frequently, a Marine close air support mission was a desperate final attempt to thwart an enemy attack.

Some of my South Vietnam missions were "milk-run" missions, or TPQ-10 missions. These sorties were under the control of a ground controller who had the coordinates of a target in a computer. We would receive a vector to the target and be directed to release our ordnance when the TPQ-10 computer computed the solution. I was

---

19   FAC - Forward Air Controller: normally an Air Force Officer in a small aircraft, but also included Army and Marine aviators as well.

20   Snake - Snake Eye: general purpose bombs fitted with fins which deployed after launch to retard the descent to the ground target. 'Nape': napalm. Navy aircraft were precluded from carrying napalm weapons because of the great potential for fire aboard a carrier in the event of an accident.

told these were fairly accurate missions but we were bus drivers under control of the ground controller.

Missions under an airborne FAC were more exciting and challenging. Frequently we would check in with a FAC who would fire smoke rounds to mark the target to us or advise us to watch his aircraft while he descended over enemy forces to draw fire. We could always visually acquire the target by following the tracers back to their source. It goes without saying that most FACs were extremely courageous.

I remember one night mission for which we were fragged for air-to-ground over South Vietnam. It was a night mission. We were a two-aircraft element. Lead was flown by LT CDR Jack Batzler and his RIO LT JG Don Skinner. After launch we climbed out on our assigned radial and rendezvoused with our Lead at the tanker. Both aircraft received two thousand pounds of fuel. We then proceeded to the vicinity of Tiger Island and orbited in the vicinity waiting to be handed over to the control of an airborne FAC. We continued to orbit for a lengthy period of time frequently advising our ground controller of our diminishing fuel status. As we approached bingo fuel we were given a vector over South Vietnam and told to change frequency and check in with our airborne FAC. We did so and proceeded under his directions to the North West area of South Vietnam, in the vicinity of the Ho Chi Minh Trail through which North Vietnam supplied its forces in the South.

He advised us of his location from a TACAN in Laos and told us where to take station. After arrival we reported a visual on his blinking navigation lights which he turned on to assist in locating him placing him at risk of enemy fire. He advised us of a lengthy convoy of trucks accompanied by truck mounted 23-millimeter anti-aircraft batteries which he wanted very badly to destroy. I assumed these trucks recently arrived into the South via the Ho Chi Minh Trail.

The FAC ordered us to take orbit at the location, each aircraft across the circle from the other. He advised Lead to begin his attack on his command. He advised us that he was going to descend over the convoy to draw fire which would mark the target.

I watched in fascination as the blinking light descended into the darkness. Suddenly there was a red stream of tracer rounds appearing which clearly marked the convoy. I was also able to see headlights with the upper half blackened out on some thirty trucks. At the FAC's command, Lead rolled in. Bob and I completed our checklist and watched while we climbed to an altitude of about twenty thousand feet. We couldn't actually see Lead because his lights were out. We, as the wing man, had our exterior lights on bright and flash. We saw a terrific bright flash as Lead's ordnance exploded and heard Lead report he was off the target, at bingo fuel, and was proceeding to Home Plate. The FAC acknowledged the call with obvious disappointment in his voice and advised that Lead had missed the target too far to the west and the convoy was continuing unscathed. He gave us directions on where to place our bombs in relation to where Lead's struck.

Bob acknowledged and kept a visual on the area. I was inside the cockpit. I reminded Bob to turn off our tail light. The enemy could now hear us but could not see us and would fire at our sound. We were flying at 425-knots so he would have to pull the right amount of lead to strike us. Bob rolled almost inverted from about twenty thousand feet and began a 30-degree dive angle. I provided him altitude and air speed information as well as dive angle information since he was flying visually on the target and could not look inside the cockpit. At a thousand feet above release I gave him a "Standby!" Then at release altitude, "Mark, pull up, jink!" We pulled off and I gave him a vector which would take us back over the South, avoiding the North, to Tiger Island. As we rolled on the heading and completed our checklist, the FAC came over the air. He was ecstatic!

"A direct hit!" he exclaimed. "You got the entire convoy! I'm not receiving any fire as I fly over the position."

"Roger," I responded. "Thanks. We're at bingo fuel and have to leave. Enjoyed working with you."

"Ditto," he replied. "Good job!"

We switched frequencies and checked in as we navigated to the ship. Recovery was uneventful. Back in the Ready Room Bob grinned as I told our squadron mates that he had been credited with killing an entire convoy. It was a grin of humility. It wasn't easy to realize we had been the direct cause of so many human deaths. We were grateful, however, when we also realized that we had saved the lives of Americans and South Vietnamese.

One of my favorite missions was Photo Escort. On our first cruise in 1968 the photo birds were the North American A5 Vigilante. These birds had the strategic nuclear strike mission for the Navy until the Boomer Boats[21] became operational and were designed for long range penetration of the Soviet Homeland. They were sleek, unencumbered with racks or other external stores. They had the same J-79 engines as the F 4. However, because the nuclear strike mission no longer existed they used the bomb bay for fuel storage which gave them an extended range. They were so clean they could out accelerate a Phantom. On Photo Recce missions over North Vietnam the Phantom would have to "cut the corner" on the flight route to keep up with the Vigilante who was using all available speed in military rated thrust to conduct the mission.

A variant of the Photo Recce mission was to use the Vigilante's Side Looking Radar (SLR) for a mission into Laos, just west of the boundary with North Vietnam. The flight would enter South Vietnam just south of the DMZ using Tiger Island as an IP, fly along the DMZ until into Laotian airspace, then fly northwest along the Laotian - North Vietnamese border. As the flight flew northwest, the Vigilante's SLR would observe and capture the North Vietnamese movement south along the Ho Chi Minh Trail ferrying men and supplies to the South. This information, when loaded off the Vigilante on return to the carrier would be used to frag the next day's missions using Navy, Air Force and Marine Corps assets.

Because the mission was a long-range mission the Phantom would be refueled right after launch and would always have fuel reserved for it if needed upon return over the Gulf of Tonkin.

Launch was always scheduled at night with a programmed recovery aboard the boat just before sunrise affording the pilots the ability to log a night trap in visual conditions. The mission was a good deal all the way! The squadron schedules officer ensured everyone had an opportunity to fly these missions.

---

[21] Boomer Boats - the nuclear powered submarines with the Polaris, later Trident, nuclear armed intercontinental ballistic missiles (ICBMs).

I remember a typical mission. We would brief with the Vigilante aircrew either in their Ready Room or ours. The Bombardier/ Navigator, or B/N, would have plotted the route. I transferred his navigation points and route to my chart. I noticed he carefully avoided all known SAM sites as currently plotted in IOIC. I believe the A5 had the SINS, the Shipboard Inertial Navigation System, which the carrier had with instant navigation from the satellites. The A5 had a receptacle which would provide an update from the ship's system immediately prior to launch. I can't remember if the A5 was like the A6 Intruder and could update off the satellite while airborne. In any event, the navigation part of the mission was never a problem.

We would typically launch late in the cycle, climb out and rendezvous with the tanker, taking on two thousand pounds of fuel which would top us off. We always insured fuel transfer worked. Rendezvous with both the tanker and the Vigilante was on radar. Typically, the tanker was on a heading that would take us south towards Tiger Island and the rendezvous point with the Vigilante was south so that we could make a running rendezvous, saving fuel. This was an exact science!

After rendezvous we would take wing position flying off the Vigilante whose exterior lights were set at dim and steady. The Phantom would continue on bright and flash. The mission was flown at thirty-thousand feet so the risk of visual acquisition was slim. Airspeed was at a comfortable three hundred knots until over Laos at which time the flight increased speed to 420 knots, the Phantom's corner velocity or maneuvering speed.

The flight proceeded south. Tiger Island was prominent on the radar and I used it to update the navigation computer. By this time, all systems had been checked sweet, including the missiles and fuel transfer. As we approached Tiger Island and turned to the west to fly south of the DMZ, we could see the lights of South Vietnam. We could also see sporadic fire fights occurring. I picked up frequent flights of helicopters and/or other tactical aircraft on attack and support missions on radar. We had our own discrete frequency, but occasionally we could hear transmissions on military guard frequency of units under attack or aircraft going down. To the North the land mass was darkened. Nothing was visible. The contrast was stark.

One of the transmissions we would occasionally hear on guard was the Arc Light missions of the B52 bombers dropping their tons of bombs from thirty-thousand feet, our altitude. The B52 is such a huge aircraft that it is very prominent on the Phantom's radar and can be easily seen. We were under orders not to attempt to lock full systems on the BUFF (big, ugly, fat fellow) because that would make the aircrews nervous. The ECM operator aboard the BUFF had the capability of slamming the Phantom's antenna so hard against the stops that it could cause a hydraulic leak in the utility system, definitely not a good thing. I never did encounter any BUFFS on my photo Recce missions over Laos.

We completed the combat checklist so we would occasionally receive radar homing and warning (RHAW) indications of various radars painting and tracking us while over South Vietnam. Once we were in Laotian airspace and turned the corner on a northwesterly heading the RHAW was normally quiet. North Vietnamese search radars would frequently paint us on our journey but never actually locked-on in a fire control mode since our distance from the SAM sites normally exceeded maximum range of the batteries' missiles. However, it was possible that they could move the site to a different location so we kept our vigilance up.

Bob flew instrument wing on the A5 but it was not demanding since we maintained a constant altitude and our course changes were gradual. I always gave him advance notice of an impending course change. My job was to navigate, keep up a search of airborne targets on the scope (any airborne target would normally be hostile at this time of the morning), keep the Vigilante in sight, and keep track of our fuel, both remaining and required for the return trip. This afforded me plenty of time to look out the cockpit at the area below us. When we first turned to the northwesterly heading we could see the plentiful lights of Thailand. Although not very numerous, the lights in Laos were clearly visible. North Vietnam remained completely blacked out and dark.

I could also paint cumulus cloud build-up on the radar and occasionally see lightning flashes off to the distance. I would occasionally allow myself the luxury of reflecting about this alien land and what exactly we were doing here. Sometimes I wondered what it would be like if we had to eject over Laos. What would we find on the ground? There were some friendly people in the area but I anticipated that most would be unfriendly or hostile.

Always, the reflection from the searching radar would illuminate the cockpit with its green glow. This illumination, together with the dim red lights of the instrument panel, helped to impregnate the entire scenario with a surreal quality. I could see the silhouette of the Vigilante, its sleek black form penetrating the night with a grace and beauty that belied its destructive potential. I could only imagine what the average North Vietnamese or Laotian would think about us high overhead of his land and home, alien invaders of his airspace. The North Vietnamese, of course, had the potential to strike with SAMS or MiGs which served as a touchstone of reality lest I wandered too far off my required vigilance.

The great majority of our strike missions were over North Vietnam. Typically, we would launch on a day-light Rolling Thunder mission in a two plane element. More often than naught we would tank immediately after launch, join up and proceed to the target in combat spread formation at a speed of 450 knots. I don't ever remember having to abort a flight because of a fuel transfer malfunction or electronic countermeasure suit malfunction which spoke highly of our maintenance crews. We would carry a strike ordnance load of five hundred pound general purpose bombs and/or five inch Zuni rocket pod launchers (three rockets to a pod). These Zuni rockets had the same punch as the five inch gun of a destroyer so they were a considerable force for the North Vietnamese to reckon with.

We very seldom spoke on the radio unless necessary. Flying over the beach into North Vietnam was always cause for a rush of adrenalin and focused concentration of the mission. There was always much to do and extraordinarily little time for sightseeing but a vast expanse of the country was always visible from the cockpit. I remember North

Vietnam as a green, flat country in the eastern portion covered by many rivers and deltas, similar to the coast of southeast Georgia. The country was alive, however, with electronic transmissions which caused a constant chatter in our headsets from the RHAW gear. Although not ever present, flak could frequently be seen, not always aimed at us but other attack aircraft operating in the vicinity.

The flying was pleasant given the constant threat against us. One could look out from the cockpit at the North Vietnamese countryside and a scenic country. The many rice paddies bespoke of a fertile land with a people who have lived on it for over two-thousand years. The North Vietnamese had fought, among others, the Chinese, the French, the Japanese, and now the Americans. I wondered what type of lasting impression, if any, the Americans would make on this country.

The carrier and its air wing quickly reached peak efficiency so operations were like clockwork. After a daylight VFR mission aircraft would return home entering the break in pre-arranged order and make daylight carrier recovery with no more radio calls than the "ball" call, indicating to the ship that the aircraft was in the final approach phase, or in the groove, in landing configuration with gear, flaps and hook down. Sometimes an entire recovery of some twenty-five to thirty aircraft would be completed with just the ball calls.

Once back aboard the boat the aircraft and crew came under the total control of the flight deck personnel who were lean and skilled from constant non-stop hours of operations. Error free conduct of the extremely complex carrier operations was the norm, although exceptions did occur. Life aboard the boat was a series of watches, mission preparation, routine maintenance and care of our people. There was plenty of time for discussion and contemplation and being homesick. Each day, however, inevitably brought with it another launch into skies and combat.

Yet, it was always a pleasure to fly, to reach up into the heavens in the magnificent Phantom. Sometimes the cumulus clouds would reach to almost fifty-thousand feet and form a spectacular backdrop to the green river-crossed land below. My memory of Vietnam was one of great beauty in deadly circumstance. The Phantom carried with it almost certain death and destruction to the enemy who pitted his every resource to our destruction. Yet this sleek war-bird never failed me but brought me back time after time, mission after mission, to the ship for at least temporary respite from the strain of combat. I was given the opportunity to do my duty in the service of my country. This beautiful machine took me to war and brought me home safely. I could ask no more of it.

PHOTO GALLERY

ENTERPRISE FIRE

FAMILY

Marriage Savannah, GA Jan 7, 1967

Family Christmas 1968

Juley on the beach in Hawaii 1969

151

Juley aboard Enterprise 1968

Printed in the United States
by Baker & Taylor Publisher Services